Tourism and Public Policy

Routledge Topics in Tourism

Series Adviser:
Stephen Page, Massey University Albany, Auckland

Routledge Topics in Tourism offers a fresh, concise grounding in key themes in tourism and leisure. Each book in the series acts as a succinct and stimulating introduction to a particular topic and provides:

- comprehensive discussions of concepts
- international case studies
- key point summaries
- short questions for discussion

This series will be an excellent resource for student of tourism and leisure courses at first-year undergraduate and diploma levels.

Titles include:

Tourism Destination Management
Eric Laws, Christ Church College, Canterbury

People in Tourism
Tom Baum, University of Buckingham

Urban Tourism
Stephen Page, Massey University Albany, Auckland

Transport for Tourism
Stephen Page, Massey University Albany, Auckland

Colin Michael Hall and John M. Jenkins

Tourism and
Public Policy

London and New York

First published 1995
by Routledge
11 New Fetter Lane, London EC4P 4EE

Simultaneously published in the USA and Canada
by Routledge
29 West 35th Street, New York, NY 10001

Typeset in Times by Florencetype Ltd, Stoodleigh, Devon
Printed and bound in Great Britain by Biddles Ltd,
Guildford and King's Lynn

British Library Cataloguing in Publication Data
A catalogue record of this book is available from the British Library

Library of Congress Cataloging in Publication Data
Hall, C. M. (C. Michael)
    Tourism and public policy / Colin Michael Hall and John M. Jenkins.
      p. cm. – (Routledge topics in tourism)
    Includes bibliographical references and index.
    ISBN 0–415–11354–7
      1. Tourist trade and state. I. Jenkins, John M. (John Michael), 1961–
II. Title.   III. Series.
G155.A1H348   1995
338.4′79104–dc20   95–7642
                                                                     CIP

ISBN 0–415–11354–7

To Cathie, Edward and Phoebe;
The Wandering Islands
and
Dave Crag

Contents

Figures

Tables

Preface

Academic research, as with tourism policy, is a value laden and political activity. Unfortunately, despite the recognition of the importance of government and tourist organisations, the field of tourism studies has developed with little attention to, and understanding of, the real significance of tourism policy. Too often we are passive in our acceptance of government activity in tourism, which is perhaps a reflection of the willingness of tourism researchers to accept contemporary institutional arrangements. There is a need for much debate and argument over tourism policy-making and the study of tourism policies. The role that power, values and interests play in tourism policy and tourism research requires far greater attention than has hitherto been the case.

The present book is designed to provide an introduction to the study of tourism public policy. The book aims to introduce to students some of the key concepts and issues that affect our understanding of the policy process. Therefore, the chapters are organised around several critical concepts: institutional arrangements, values, interest groups, power, and evaluation. The book utilises the extensive policy studies literature to provide an overview of potential directions for further studies in tourism. The book explicitly questions the prevalence of the fact–value dichotomy which pervades much of the field of tourism studies. In other words, any 'facts' are open to question according to one's values, position and power, and can be interpreted and used accordingly. In the same way, we openly acknowledge that the contents of the book reflect our own personal values in terms of the study of tourism public policy, and readers will accept, reject and utilise aspects of the book that reflect their values and interests. Indeed, we openly encourage argument and debate because it will enhance our knowledge of the political processes which surround tourism.

Many people have helped in the writing of this book, some unwittingly! Dick Butler, Jenni Craik, Margaret Johnston, Geoff Kearsley, Les Killion, Peter Murphy, Steve Page, Kathryn Pavlovich, Doug Pearce, John Pigram, Tony Sorensen, Jim Walmsley, Bernie Walsh, John Warhurst, and Josette Wells all provided valuable academic stimulation. For their interest and moral support, particularly during key policy events, we would also like to thank Ann Applebee, Julie Barbatano, Dave Crag, Stuart Christopherson, Helen Gladstones, Chris Hamon, Julie Hodges, Steve Hollë, Nicolle Lavelle, Treve McCarthy, Jenny Millea, Christine Palywoda, Christine Petersen, Jacqui Pinkava, Isabelle Sebastian, Brian Stoddart, Sue Wright. Billy Joel, Van Morrison, Rolling Stones (John), Neil and Tim Finn, Indigo Girls, Sarah McLachlan, This Mortal Coil, David Wilcox, and Lucinda Williams (Michael) also greatly assisted with the completion of this work.

Francesca Weaver of Routledge provided valuable support. The provision of research funding from the Australian Research Council, University of Canberra Research Grant Scheme, Centre for Tourism and Leisure Policy Research, the University of Central Queensland, the Association for Canadian Studies in Australia and New Zealand and Canadian Airlines International assisted in the undertaking of research which contributed to this book. Finally, we would like to thank our families and friends for their love and support over the past years.

C. Michael Hall
John M. Jenkins

1
Introduction: studying tourism public policy

> Policy analysis is one activity for which there can be no fixed program,
> for policy analysis is synonymous with creativity, which may be
> stimulated by theory and sharpened by practice . . .
>
> (Wildavsky 1979: 3)

Tourism is the world's largest industry, and is expected to continue to
grow and maintain that status well into the twenty-first century. The
tourist industry is a major economic, environmental and socio-cultural
force, and 'a highly political phenomenon' (Richter 1989: 2). According
to Peck and Lepie (1989: 216), 'the nature of tourism in any given
community is the product of complex interrelated economic and political
factors, as well as particular, geographic and recreational features that
attract "outsiders" '. The economics of tourism (e.g. see Bull 1991),
its geographical features (e.g. see Pearce 1987) and recreational characteristics (e.g. see Ryan 1991) have received considerable attention.
However, studies of the politics of tourism, and particularly of the public
policy process, are scant (Hall 1994a). Indeed, the implications of the
politics of tourism 'have been only rarely perceived and almost nowhere
fully understood' (Richter 1989: 2). In short, tourism has an urgent need
for public policy studies.

Public policy is the focal point of government activity. Tourism has
become an integral part of the machinery of many modern governments, and of many government programmes in both developed and
lesser developed countries (Lea 1988; Pearce 1989, 1992; Richter 1989;

Williams and Shaw 1988; Harrison 1992; Craig-Smith and French 1994; Hall 1994a, 1995). At the same time, several authors have noted increasing scepticism and uneasiness about the effectiveness of government, and the intended consequences and impacts of much government policy (e.g. Ham and Hill 1984; Hogwood and Gunn 1984; Dye 1992), including tourism public policy (e.g. Richter, 1989; Craik 1991; Jenkins 1993a; Hall 1994a, 1995). For instance, Richter (1989: 21) reported that 'critics of current tourism policies are becoming aware and are more than a little cynical about the excesses and "mistakes" occasioned by national tourism development schemes'. Little wonder tourism policy analysis, like other arenas of public policy inquiry before it, is slowly coming to centre 'on a search for patterns and relationships that explain as well as describe the actions of government' (Atkinson and Chandler 1983: 3).

Studies of tourism public policy must go beyond describing what governments do. However, as a relatively new area of scholarly inquiry, there is little agreement about how tourism public policies should be studied and the reasons underpinning such studies. One of the most detailed explanations as to why greater attention should be devoted to the study of public policy was presented by Dye (1992) who argued that public policy can be studied for three primary reasons. First, public policy can be studied for purely scientific reasons so as to gain an understanding of the causes and consequences of policy decisions, and to improve our knowledge about society. In this instance, public policy can be viewed as a dependent variable *or* an independent variable. If policy is viewed as a dependent variable, the critical focus for inquiry becomes 'what socio-economic [or environmental forces] and political system characteristics operate to shape the content of policy' (Dye 1992: 4). If tourism public policy is viewed as an independent variable, then the central question becomes what impact does public policy have on society (the environment) and on the political system. Second, public policy can be studied for professional reasons in order to understand the causes and consequences of policy. Thus, we might apply social science knowledge to the solution of practical problems, and feed that knowledge into the political process. Third, public policy can be studied for political purposes so as 'to ensure that the nation adopts the "right" policies to achieve the "right" goals' (Dye 1992: 5). This latter focus raises the critical issues of defining what is 'right', and identifying by whom 'right' is determined. Yet, if studies are undertaken for purely political purposes, these issues may not even concern the analyst (see Chapters 5 and 6).

In this book, we encourage students to undertake tourism public policy studies in order to understand the causes and consequences of policies, decisions, and actions. Public policy cannot remain independent of the political process and cannot be value free. We all hold particular views of the world. As discussed later in this chapter and in Chapter 3, those views affect how we act out our lives, and therefore how we conduct our research. Moreover, no matter what our beliefs, and no matter what the outcomes of our studies of policies, in the hands of politicians, bureaucrats and policy interests, the intended outcomes of our research may alter drastically as others place their interpretations on research methods and findings.

The study of tourism policy offers the opportunity to examine many topics which should be of interest not only to the tourist industry, government agencies and students of tourism, but to researchers working within and on the boundaries of many other disciplines (e.g. economics, geography, history, sociology). These topics include:

- the political nature of the tourism policy-making process;
- public participation in the tourism planning and policy process;
- the sources of power in tourism policy-making;
- the exercise of choice by public servants in complex policy environments; and
- perceptions as to the effectiveness of tourism policies.

The remainder of this chapter introduces the reader to many issues concerning tourism public policy studies. The following section identifies the potential significance of tourism policy studies, and provides definitions of tourism, public policy, and tourism public policy. The second section identifies several approaches to the study of tourism policy. It presents a model of the policy process, and a framework for the study of public policy. The third section provides an outline of the various chapters of the book.

The tourism policy process is not well understood. Therefore, this book seeks to provide a brief, yet comprehensive framework for investigating the forces that shape tourism public policies, and the intended and unintended consequences of tourism policies in terms of their impacts on communities and on the political system. For those readers expecting absolute solutions to tourism policy problems, read no further. This book does not attempt to establish a rational decision-making framework for policy-makers. A basic assumption in the writing of this book is that description and explanation should precede policy prescription.

The significance of tourism policy studies

[I]f the first signs of trouble are perceived, it is easy to find a solution; but if one lets trouble develop, the medicine will be too late, because the malady will have become incurable. And what physicians say about consumptive diseases is also true of this matter, namely, that at the beginning of the illness, it is easy to treat but difficult to diagnose but, if it has not been diagnosed and treated at an early stage, as time passes it becomes easy to diagnose but difficult to treat . . . if one recognises political problems early . . . they may be resolved quickly, but if they are not recognised, and left to develop so that everyone recognises them, there is no longer any remedy.

(Machiavelli 1988: 11)

According to Kosters (1984: 612), 'if a multi-disciplinary tourism science develops without the necessary ingredient of political analysis, it will remain imperfect and incomplete'. Tourism public policies are enmeshed in a dynamic, ongoing process, and it has become increasingly evident that governments struggle to comprehend the tourism industry, its impacts and future, and how they should intervene (Pearce 1992; Jenkins 1993a, 1994). Until recently, basic information concerning visitor flows and tourist expenditures have been lacking, and in some countries and regions such data are still far from comprehensive or even accurate. In other words, quality information concerning the tourist industry is limited. We might even hypothesise that there is an element of inexperience in tourism policy formulation and implementation as much government activity in the tourist industry is relatively recent as compared with other traditional concerns of government, such as economics, manufacturing and social welfare. These two factors in and of themselves suggest that tourism public policies are likely to be *ad hoc* and incremental. Nevertheless, perceptions of the tourist industry in terms of its economic, environmental and social impacts and future have advanced rapidly.

The importance and relative influence of tourism, and particularly its economic impacts, are reflected in its dramatic growth in global political prominence during the 1970s and 1980s. In developed countries, the state, and government itself, has many responsibilities including defence, economic development, education, health, and law and order. These particular responsibilities that rest mainly with government have been the subject of much public policy inquiry. However, tourism has only relatively recently emerged as an obvious commitment and important consideration in the public sector (Hall 1994a). As a result, analysis of tourism policies is often constrained by:

- the lack of consensus concerning definitions of such fundamental concepts as 'tourism', 'tourist', and the 'tourist industry';
- the lack of recognition given to tourism policy-making processes and the consequent lack of comparative data and case studies;
- the lack of well-defined analytical and theoretical frameworks; and
- the limited amount of quantitative and qualitative data.

Moreover, any study of tourism public policies must come to terms with the multitude of definitions of 'public policy', an issue to which the discussion now turns.

What is public policy?

Public policy-making is first and foremost a political activity. Public policy is influenced by the economic, social, and cultural characteristics of society, as well as by the formal structures of government and other features of the political system (see Self 1985). Policy-making involves the economic, physical and social/political environments in a process of action and reaction over time (Barrett and Fudge 1981). Policy is therefore a consequence of the political environment, values and ideologies, the distribution of power, institutional frameworks, and of decision-making processes (Simeon 1976) (see Figure 1.1).

Given the interaction of numerous forces in the policy-making process (e.g. individuals, agencies, laws, perceptions, ideas, choices, processes and the distribution of power), it is not surprising to find that there is little agreement in public policy studies as to what public policy is, how to identify it, and how to clarify it (Ham and Hill 1984; Pal 1992). Several definitions of public policy have been put forward (Table 1.1), and a number are critically analysed by such authors as Jenkins (1978), Anderson (1984) and Dye (1992). A common element in those definitions is that 'public policies stem from governments or public authorities. A policy is deemed a public policy not by virtue of its impact on the public, but by virtue of its source' (Pal 1992: 3).

For the purpose of this book, public policy 'is whatever governments choose to do or not to do' (Dye 1992: 2). This definition covers government action, inaction, decisions and non-decisions as it implies a deliberate choice between alternatives. For a policy to be regarded

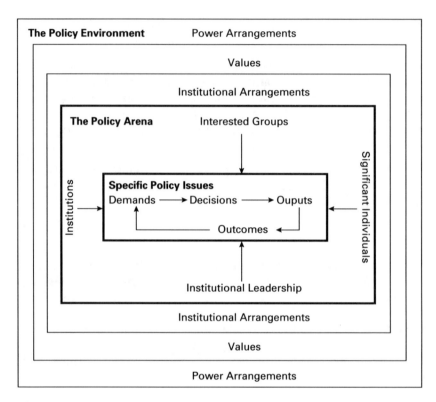

Figure 1.1 Elements in the tourism policy-making process
Source: Hall (1994a)

as public policy, at the very least it must have been processed, even if only authorised or ratified, by public agencies. This is an important caveat because it means that the 'policy may not have been significantly developed within the framework of government' (Hogwood and Gunn 1984: 23). Pressure groups, community leaders, street-level bureaucrats and others working inside and outside the 'rules of the game' established by the state – and more specifically government – influence and perceive public policies in significant and often markedly different ways. As Cunningham (1963: 229) suggested 'policy is like the elephant – you recognise it when you see it but cannot easily define it'. Cunningham's statement is significant in that it implicitly acknowledges the numerous approaches which policy studies can take – an issue addressed later in this chapter.

Table 1.1 Definitions of public policy

Public policy is 'A set of related decisions taken by a political actor or group of actors concerning the selection of goals and the means of achieving them within a specified situation where these decisions should, in principle, be within the power of these actors to achieve' (Roberts 1971: 152–153, in Jenkins 1978: 15)

Public policy 'is the relationship of a government unit to its environment' (Eyestone 1971: 18, in Anderson 1984: 2)

Public policies are those policies developed by government bodies and officials (Anderson 1984: 3)

Public policy is all the courses of action carried out by the authorities. The authorities are those who have the chief means of physical force at their disposal. In Australia that is the same as saying that the authorities are those who occupy parliamentary, executive and judicial offices provided for in the Australian and State Constitutions. So public policy is what is done in their official capacity by the Governor-General, governors, prime ministers, premiers, other ministers, parliaments and courts and all other members of offices, bureaux, directorates, services, forces, organisations, branches, divisions or whatever they are called who work under them (Forward 1974: 1)

Public policy is whatever governments choose to do or not to do (Dye 1978; 1992)

For a policy to be regarded as public policy, it must to some degree have been generated or at least processed within the framework of governmental procedures, influences and organizations (Hogwood and Gunn 1984: 24)

Public Policy is '*a course of action or inaction chosen by public authorities to address a given problem or interrelated set of problems*' (Pal 1992: 2)

What is tourism public policy?

Any consideration of what constitutes tourism public policy must also encompass an appropriate definition of tourism. However, accomplishing such a task is not easy. The previous section mentioned that there is no universally accepted definition of public policy. Similarly, according to Smith (1988: 180), tourism 'practitioners must learn to accept the myriad of [tourism] definitions and to understand and respect the reasons for those differences'. On the other hand, authors such as Leiper (1979), argue for the development of a single, comprehensive and widely accepted definition of tourism. We hold little hope for the latter. The tourist industry is diverse, fragmented and dynamic, and it can be studied at a number of levels and from many perspectives. For the purpose of this book, tourism is defined as 'the sum of the phenomena and relationships arising from the interaction of tourists, business suppliers, host governments, and host communities in the process of attracting and hosting these tourists and other visitors' (McIntosh and Goeldner 1990: 4). That said, tourism public policy is whatever governments choose to do or not to do with respect to tourism. This leaves a wide net for tourism policy researchers. The study of tourism public policy will necessarily be determined by the researcher in each case, and wherever public policy is seen to affect tourism.

Overview of approaches to the study of public policy: implications for tourism

Public policy is a separate academic discipline in its own right. It is an important area of academic scholarship that generates much debate, research, and literature. Interest in public policy research has grown considerably since the 1960s. That growth began in the United States and Britain as social scientists were attracted to the applied, socially relevant, multi-disciplinary, integrative, and problem-directed nature of policy analysis (Hogwood and Gunn 1984). Pleas for more policy relevance (Easton 1965), the speedy growth of public policy activity and government intervention after the Second World War, and the failure of many policy initiatives also contributed to the growth in public policy research.

A conceptual understanding of the policy-making process is fundamental to the analysis of public policy in any policy arena, including tourism, because policies imply theories (Brooks 1993). As Pressman and Wildavsky (1973) expressed so cogently:

> Whether stated explicitly or not, policies point to a chain of causation between initial conditions and future consequences. If X, then Y. Policies become programs when, by authoritative action, the initial conditions are created. X now exists. Programs make the theories operational by forging the first link in the causal chain connecting actions to objectives. Given X, we act to attain Y.
>
> (Pressman and Wildavsky 1973: xv)

Majone (1980a) similarly argued that:

> policies may be viewed as theories from two related but different perspectives . . . they can be seen as an analyst's rational reconstruction of a complex sequence of events . . . they can [also] be seen from the point of view of actions, as doctrines which evolve from past decisions and actions, giving them stability and internal coherence.
>
> (Majone 1980a: 178)

Public policy theory serves as the basis for explaining decision-making and policy-making processes, and for identifying the causal links between events. 'A theory serves to direct one's attention to particular features of the world, thus performing the essential task of distinguishing the significant from the irrelevant' (Brooks 1993: 28). Yet, the importance, use and relevance of particular public policy theories often rest on the research philosophy and world views of the analyst or those who designed the study. Put simply, *people* decide on definitions and theories that are relevant to the scope and features of the policy process under investigation. *People* tend to view policies and policy-making through their own world views, and these will, more or less, dictate a study's outcomes (e.g. see Allison 1971; Brooks 1993; Majone 1980b, 1989; Quade 1980; Mitchell 1989). 'Problem solving for the policy analyst is as much a matter of creating a problem (1) worth solving from a social perspective and (2) capable of being solved with the resources at hand, as it is of converging to a solution when given a problem' (Wildavsky 1979: 388). Policy analysis 'is synonymous with creativity' (Wildavsky 1979: 3) and is akin to an 'art' or 'craft' (Wildavsky 1979; Majone 1980a, 1980b, 1989). Both Majone and Wildavsky see policy analysis as an activity for which there can be no fixed programme. Theory is the tool of the artisan. Description, analysis and explanation, and the use of appropriate theory to help explain events, are necessarily influenced by the researcher's ability and desire to manipulate data, and by his/her intellectual bias. Different theoretical perspectives, e.g. pluralist, elitist, Marxist, corporatist (Ham and Hill 1984); or, pluralist, public choice and Marxist (Brooks 1993), while not mutually exclusive, conceptualise the policy process in distinct ways. Moreover, theories can be distinguished from one another by their *level of analysis*, in terms of their *world view*, and by the *methods* they typically employ in studying public policy (Brooks 1993). Each perspective therefore differs in its assumptions about political conflict, the appropriate level of analysis, and the research method. Researchers freely choose their perspective(s).

The above situation has contributed to the lack of a dominant or coherent approach in public policy studies (e.g. see Jenkins 1978; Davis *et al.* 1993; Brooks 1993). Nevertheless, policy research, and, indeed, research throughout the sciences, can be built up on two main types of theory: that which adopts prescriptive models and that which adopts descriptive models (Mitchell 1989; Brooks 1993).

'Prescriptive or normative models seek to demonstrate how policy-making should occur relative to pre-established standards', whereas 'descriptive models document the way in which the policy process actually occurs' (Mitchell 1989: 264). Prescriptive (normative) models serve as a guide to an ideal situation. However, a descriptive approach is preferred when exploring a new territory in a particular policy arena. Descriptive (positive) theories/models give rise to explanations about what happened during the decision-making and policy-making processes. They help analysts to understand the effects that choice, power, perception, values and process have on policy-making. In other words, although prescriptive models are deductive, one cannot deduce in the absence of prior knowledge. This book advocates a descriptive approach in the hope that, among other things, it will provide an information base for future decision-makers.

The following section explains how studies of tourism public policy might proceed. The discussion first presents a useful and simple model of the policy process and indicates broadly the different levels at which forces on policy operate. It then proceeds to establish a framework for analysing those levels and influences.

Studying public policy: linking the macro, meso and micro levels of policy analysis

the focus of political science is shifting to *public policy* – to the *description and explanation of the causes and consequences of government activity*. This involves a description of the content of public policy; an assessment of the impact of environmental forces on the content of public policy; an analysis of the effect of various institutional arrangements and political processes on public policy; an inquiry into the consequences of various public policies for the political system; and an evaluation of the [processes and] impact of public policies on society, in terms of both expected and unexpected consequences.

(Dye 1978: 5).

Public policy is a process as policies are formulated and implemented in dynamic environments where there is a complex pattern of decisions, actions, interaction, reaction and feedback. Figure 1.2 presents a systems model of the policy process which has been amended from earlier work by Easton (1965). This model is a systemic one which implies 'that public policy is best understood by considering the operation of a political system in its environment and by examining how such a system maintains itself and changes over time' (Jenkins 1978: 21). The model, as Jenkins suggests, is but a guide to thought

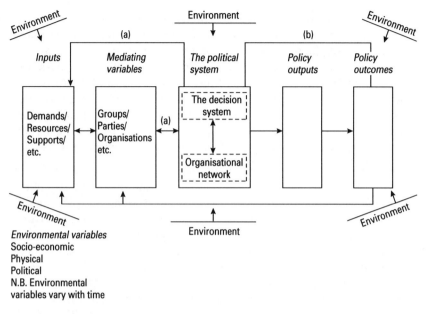

Figure 1.2 Amended systems model of the policy-making process

Source: Jenkins (1978: 22)

because it is grossly oversimplified. However, this should not be viewed as a major criticism in the context of present knowledge of the public policy process. Encompassing 'the reality of public policy-making in one systematic interactive and operational whole is probably beyond the wit of man' (Spann and Curnow 1975: 460).

The dynamics of the policy process, and thus public policy inquiry, can be so complex that it is often difficult, and perhaps even pointless, to become engrossed in trying to distinguish between policy formulation and implementation. Such distinctions in the policy process are, at times, unfounded. Policy formulation and implementation are difficult to separate on a consistent basis because policy is often formulated as it is implemented and vice versa. The upper levels of the machinery of government may not know when the bureaucracy is formulating or implementing policy, and both may lack reliable information on both the policy arena in question, and the ensuing decisions, actions and policy outcomes. In some circumstances, the bureaucracy can work independently of government policy, and lower level bureaucrats can defy authoritative directions (see Chapter 2).

Specifying the contribution of any study of tourism public policy will be complicated by the use of concepts and ideas drawn from many traditional disciplines (geography, economics, history, law, urban and regional planning, political science, psychology, public administration, sociology, and social psychology). Much of the interest and difficulty in studying tourism public policy will perhaps be realised in its propensity to disrupt, much less traverse, disciplinary boundaries as many authors have found in other policy arenas (e.g. Wildavsky 1979). The nature and complexity of the policy process points to the importance of

> analysing both different stages of the policy process and different levels of analysis. Precisely how many levels are investigated is likely to vary according to the nature of the enquiry being undertaken, but it can be suggested that three levels will often be appropriate. These levels are: first, the micro level of decision-making within organisations; second, the middle range analysis of policy formulation [and implementation]; and third, macroanalysis of political systems including examination of the role of the state. It is the interaction between levels which is particularly significant and problematic.
>
> (Ham and Hill 1984: 17–18)

This book encourages its readers to analyse tourism public policies at a number of interrelated levels – micro, meso (middle) and macro – over time. By linking the different levels of policy analysis, any semblance of a fact/value or policy and administration dichotomy (see Wilson 1941; Simeon 1976) in tourism policy-making is dismissed. Public policy research involves not only academic research into the policy process, but also involves growing activity in applied policy analysis, often involving contract work for government or pressure or industry groups. Such work is generally aimed at influencing public policy. A discussion of research in terms of its aims, purpose, motivations and theoretical frameworks was advanced by Hogwood and Gunn (1984) who made a very detailed distinction between research orientations. Their distinction reflects the normative/positive dichotomy: analysis for policy (prescription) and analysis of policy (description).

Gunn (1976 and 1980, in Hogwood and Gunn 1984) pointed to the different ways in which various authors have used the term policy analysis. 'Terms such as "policy analysis", "policy sciences", and "policy studies" are used by various authors in different ways and at times interchangeably' (Hogwood and Gunn 1984: 26). However, Hogwood and Gunn (1984) pointed to a fruitful way to proceed. They suggested

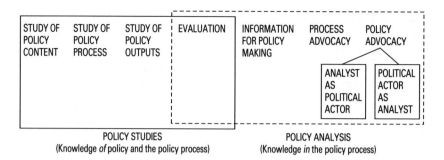

| STUDY OF POLICY CONTENT | STUDY OF POLICY PROCESS | STUDY OF POLICY OUTPUTS | EVALUATION | INFORMATION FOR POLICY MAKING | PROCESS ADVOCACY | POLICY ADVOCACY |

| | | | | | ANALYST AS POLITICAL ACTOR | POLITICAL ACTOR AS ANALYST |

POLICY STUDIES
(Knowledge *of* policy and the policy process)   POLICY ANALYSIS
(Knowledge *in* the policy process)

Figure 1.3 Types of public policy-making
Source: Hogwood and Gunn (1984: 29)

a classification of approaches (Figure 1.3) that makes it possible to distinguish more precisely between different kinds of policy analysis. The strength of such a classification is that it not only points to clearer research orientations, but it also provides for a dynamic analytical approach because the analyst can move between those more clearly defined and remarkably different orientations or conceptual frameworks. This is the approach adopted in this book.

Public policy studies will necessarily be multidimensional in focus; use an empirico-inductive research orientation; incorporate the future as well as the past; respond to study users; and explicitly incorporates values. In policy studies, the concept of 'levels of analysis' must be kept in mind, and research should try to span empiricism and theory (description and understanding/explanation).

Approach of this book: a framework for the study of tourism public policy

This book seeks to contribute to the knowledge of tourism policy-making by providing:

- a discussion which demonstrates the relevance and benefits of studies of public policy to tourism;
- an account of major issues in tourism policy; and
- an outline of the major themes which need to be considered in the study of tourism policy.

The book is divided into seven chapters. This chapter has provided an introduction to the study of tourism public policy and serves as an important precursor to the ordering of the subsequent chapters. While each chapter examines the relationship of key aspects of public policy studies to tourism, the links and dependencies between the various concepts – and their association with each of the different levels of policy analysis discussed earlier – are clearly illustrated throughout the book.

Outline of the book

Each of the following chapters addresses themes relevant to the study of tourism public policy. The themes are interlinked as it is argued that a thorough understanding of the politics of tourism cannot be had without reference to each theme. This, of course, is not meant to detract from studies which focus on a particular theme but merely to highlight the fact that the tourism policy process is complex and must be studied at a number of levels. One of the great challenges confronting tourism policy researchers is the linking of the levels of analysis. Studies which adopt a single lens view, or analyse at a particular level, are necessarily limited and partial in explaining any public policy or associated decisions and actions.

Chapter 2 examines the institutional arrangements for tourism public policy. The chapter sketches some of the major issues in the study of institutions. It discusses the role of institutional arrangements in tourism policy, explains the concept of institutions, and outlines the significance of institutional arrangements to tourism, the institutions of the state, and various components of institutional arrangements (i.e. intergovernmental and interorganisational relations). The aim of this chapter is to explain ways of setting about understanding how decisions and policies are formed within the state generally, and by government organisations specifically. It therefore demonstrates how several theoretical approaches to the study of public policy can be utilised, and how they can contribute to an understanding of tourism public policy.

Chapter 3 focuses on the values of individuals, agencies and the state in the policy process. In particular, it examines the role of values and value conflicts in tourism policy. Public policy processes, outputs and research are value-laden activities. Policy-making and policy analysis cannot be value free. Decisions and actions concerning tourism policy emerge from a political process. Values and value systems directly and indirectly affect the perceptions, attitudes, decisions and actions of actors and agencies. There are different individuals and groups within and outside tourist organisations who seek to satisfy a range of goals. In doing so, they exert force/pressure, and certain values must necessarily yield to others in power relationships which are in a state of flux.

Chapter 4 examines the role of interest groups in what is becoming an increasingly crowded and complex policy area. Exercising influence on tourism public policy through pressure groups is a legitimate activity in democracies. Groups may exercise their influence through various overt means (e.g. street marches, demonstrations, boycotts, obstructions) which may attract considerable public attention, or they may seek to undermine or negotiate with policy-makers behind closed doors. Interest groups which attempt to influence the tourism policy process range from international organisations to national agencies, state or provincial bodies, and to regional and local organisations. A wide cross-section of interest groups are therefore discussed, and the significance of their activities for tourism policy-making is outlined.

Chapter 5 provides a means of exploring who wins and who loses in tourism decision-making and policy-making. The sources of power in tourism public policy are key elements in tourism policy processes. Politics has much to do with power. Therefore, the study of power arrangements is vital in the analysis of the political impacts of tourism (Hall 1994a). However, very little is known about the power base for decisions concerning tourism policy-making, and so very little is known about how decisions are made with respect to tourism planning, development and management. Power is not centralised, but is fragmented across parties, departments, community groups and clients (Davis *et al.* 1993) which attempt to 'mobilise their bias' (Schattschneider 1960). 'Actors whose preferences prevail in conflicts over key political issues are those who exercise power in a political system. It follows that the student of power needs to analyse concrete decisions involving actors pursuing different preferences' (Ham and Hill 1984: 62). Students of tourism policy are likely to uncover overt and covert conflicts, decisions and actions in the policy process. Nondecisions may be as significant to that process as actual decisions because important issues may not even enter the decision-making process (they may be organised out).

Chapter 6 outlines the importance of constantly monitoring and evaluating the tourism public policy process. The need for more extensive evaluations of tourism public policies has been reinforced by the choices forced on politicians as the result of continuing restraints in government spending, and the resulting trade-offs among existing policy commitments. 'In the years to come, resources in both the public and the private sector will continue to be in much demand – that is, scarce. Hence, the commanding need to use them wisely' (Etzioni 1984: 7). Chapter 6 therefore defines the tasks of monitoring and evaluating tourism policies, and suggests means of conducting same.

Chapter 7 outlines potential future directions in tourism policy research and identifies key elements which require further investigation. The decisions and actions of, and networks created between, stakeholders in tourism will exert powers in different forms and with different outcomes over time.

Summary

This chapter has clarified a number of issues concerning the study of tourism public policy – definitions, concepts, models and approaches. We have argued that public policy should be analysed at several levels, but have made no attempt to institute a 'best practice' to the study of tourism policies. We doubt there is an ideal model to studying public policy, and we doubt there ever will be. 'Understanding public policy is both an art and a craft' (Dye 1992: 17), and so is making policy. The following chapters hope to provide some insights into the making and study of public policy.

Governments and their critics have become more aware of and interested in the study of the process, outcomes and impacts of tourism public policies. Hence, the evaluation of government decisions, actions and programmes, and therefore of tourism public policies, is receiving growing recognition. Complex programmes require extensive investigations to examine process, outcomes, and adjustments. Given the dynamic and sometimes turbulent environments in which most tourist organisations operate, the discretion of bureaucrats in policy implementation, the numerous interests that want a say in government policy, and the difficulties in balancing interests and values, it is argued that studies of tourism public policies might provide useful insights into who gets what, when and why in the tourism policy process, and might also make a contribution to better informed government decision-making and policy-making.

Questions for review and discussion

1 Does your country have a national tourism strategy? If so, identify and critically evaluate that strategy's stated goals and objectives. If

not, discuss the reasons as to why such a strategy does not exist, or is only in its formative stages.

2 Identify elements of the tourism policy-making environment with respect to Jenkins's (1978) model.

3 This chapter mentioned two models of the policy process, Easton's (1965) model and Jenkins's (1978) model. Can you identify other models of the policy process? How do such models compare with those presented in this chapter?

4 Discuss the importance of analysing tourism public policies at different levels.

Guide to further reading

A number of public policy texts and journal articles provide excellent introductions to the study of public policy by way of their discussions of relevant definitions, concepts, approaches, implications and future directions. Of particular note are: Anderson (1984); Brooks (1993); Davis *et al.* (1993); Dye, (1978 and 1992); Ham and Hill (1984); Hogwood and Gunn (1984). Majone (1989) and Wildavsky (1979) are both highly readable and instrumental in their discussions of policy analysis as art and craft. For more specific overviews of tourism, politics and policy see Richter (1989) and Hall (1994a).

2
The study of institutional arrangements
Constructing the rules of the game

> Institutions are both dependent variables, reflecting earlier decisions, and independent factors, conditioning the future play of political forces.
>
> (Simeon 1976: 575)

The role of institutional arrangements in tourism policy

Understanding tourism public policy demands some understanding of and reference to the institutional arrangements in which tourism policy is made. Such frameworks vary significantly between countries and between policy sectors within an individual country. 'These differences affect how political conflict is expressed, what strategies individuals and groups will employ in attempting to influence policy, and the weight that policy-makers ascribe to particular social and economic interests' (Brooks 1993: 79).

Institutional arrangements are thus one of several important factors in the tourism public policy process. They are best viewed as a filter that mediates and expresses the play of conflicting social and economic forces in society. The institutional framework mediates conflict by providing a set of rules and procedures that regulates how and where demands on public policy can be made, who has the authority to take certain decisions and actions, and how decisions and policies are implemented. It also expresses conflict in that institutions and relationships comprising the state system reflect and adapt to the broader pattern of social and economic forces (Brooks 1993). As tourism has only recently achieved notable economic and social significance, it is not surprising that tourism has only recently become an important item on the political agenda of many countries and regions.

This chapter examines broad notions concerning institutions of the state with respect to tourism. A primary focus of this chapter is to consider the policy-related aspects of institutions as they affect tourism policy-making, and on the interaction between these institutions and social forces. The institutional arrangements for tourism influence the process through which the policy agenda for tourism is shaped, the way in which tourism problems are defined and alternatives are considered, and how choices are made, and decisions and actions taken.

Concepts of the state and institutions

The state can be conceptualised as a set of officials with their own preferences and capacities to effect public policy, or in more structural terms as a relatively permanent set of *political institutions* operating in relation to civil society (Nordlinger 1981). The main institutions of the state include: the elected legislatures, government departments and authorities, the judiciary, enforcement agencies, other levels of government, government-business enterprises, regulatory authorities, and a range of para-state organisations, such as trade unions (Figure 2.1). The term 'state' thus encompasses the whole apparatus whereby a government exercises its power. It includes elected politicians, the various arms of the bureaucracy, public/civil servants, and a plethora of rules, regulations, laws, conventions and policies. The functions of the state will affect tourism policy and development to different degrees. However, the degree to which individual functions are related to particular tourism policies and decisions will depend on the specific objectives of institutions, interest groups and significant individuals relative to the policy process (Hall 1994a).

Institutions

The term 'institution' has many meanings, though there is some consensus about the importance of rules and the regulation of individual and group behaviour. For the purpose of this book, institutions are 'an established law, custom, usage, practice, organisation, or other element in the political or social life of a people; a regulative principle or

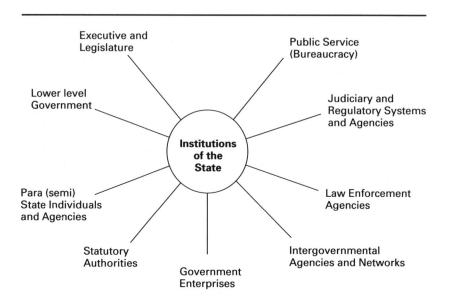

- *Executive and legislature*: e.g. systems of government, heads of state, government and opposition, minister responsible for tourism.
- *Public service (bureaucracy)*: e.g. government departments (and their staff), Departments of Tourism, tourism bureaucrats.
- *Judiciary and regulatory systems and agencies*: courts of law.
- *Law enforcement agencies*: armed forces, police, customs.
- *Intergovernmental agencies and networks*: committees, councils, conferences, networks and partnerships (formal and informal), ministerial committees on tourism.
- *Government enterprises*: trading banks, essential services (e.g. communications and transport), statutory travel and tourism promotion organisations.
- *Statutory authorities*: central banks; educational institutions (schools and higher education).
- *Para (semi) – state individuals and agencies*: media, interest groups, trade unions, peak industry bodies, tourism associations.
- *Lower levels of government*: state/provincial and local/regional governments.

Figure 2.1 Schematic structure of the state with reference to tourism

Source: Adapted from Davis *et al.* (1993)

convention subservient to the needs of an organized community or the general needs of civilization' (Scrutton 1982: 225). In short, we might think of institutions as a set of rules which may be explicit and formalised (e.g. constitutions, statutes and regulations) or implicit and informal (e.g. organisational culture, rules governing personal networks and family relationships). Thus institutions are an entity devised to order interrelationships between individuals or groups of individuals by influencing their behaviour. As a concept and as an aspect of policy-making, institutions cast a wide net; they are extensive and pervasive forces in the political system.

The significance of institutional arrangements to tourism

Institutional arrangements are an aspect of the politics of tourism which need much greater attention than has hitherto been the case. In a broad context, O'Riordan (1971) observed that:

One of the least touched upon, but possibly one of the most funda-mental, research needs in resource management [and indeed, tourism management] is the analysis of how institutional arrangements are formed, and how they evolve in response to changing needs and the existence of internal and external stress. There is growing evidence to suggest that the form, structure and operational guidelines by which resource management institutions are formed and evolve clearly affect the implementation of resource policy, both as to the range of choice adopted and the decision attitudes of the personnel involved.

(O'Riordan 1971: 135)

'Policy making is filtered through a complex institutional framework' (Brooks 1993: 79). Institutional arrangements are 'a significant research question' (Mitchell 1989: 243) for tourism which has yet to receive detailed scrutiny. In the short run, institutions 'place constraints on decision-makers and help shape outcomes by making some solutions harder, rather than by suggesting positive alternatives' (Simeon 1976: 574). As the number of check points for policy increase, so too does the potential for bargaining and negotiation. In the longer run, 'institutional arrangements may themselves be seen as policies, which, by building in to the decision process the need to consult particular groups and follow particular procedures, increase the likelihood of some kinds of decisions and reduces [sic] that of others' (Simeon 1976: 575). New government departments may be established as part of the growth in the activity and influence of government, particularly as new demands, such as environmental concerns, reach a high priority on the political agenda.

The setting up of entirely new government departments, advisory bodies or sections within the existing administration is a well established strategy on the part of governments for demonstrating loudly and clearly that 'something positive is being done' with respect to a given problem. Moreover, because public service bureaucracies are inherently conservative in terms of their approach to problem delineation and favoured mode of functioning . . . administrative restructuring, together with the associated legislation, is almost always a significant indicator of public pressure for action and change.

(Mercer 1979: 107)

Despite the importance of institutions and institutional processes to public policy, noninstitutional approaches have tended to dominate research methodologies and therefore understandings of public policy processes and the state (March and Olsen 1989, in Pal 1992: 99–100). Noninstitutional approaches are associated with five main characteristics. First, contextualism – whereby the structure and process of politics is simply the function of context which may vary according to the world views of the analyst. For example, the key contextual factor for neo-Marxists is class structure. The central point being that societal forces are assumed to affect politics, but politics is assumed to have little impact on society. Second, reductionism assumes that the outcomes of social systems are the result of microforces. Utilitarianism 'assumes that individuals behave on the basis of calculated decisions', taking rational decisions and actions on the basis of their preferences and interests. Instrumentalism gives little recognition to the importance of rituals and symbols in politics, preferring to see political action as strategic action. 'Functionalism assumes that certain patterns of interaction exist in the political system because they serve the survival needs of that system.'

In stark contrast to noninstitutional approaches, recognition of institutional arrangements for public policy highlights the fact that politics and policy-making have many distinct characteristics and dynamics that cannot simply be explained away as secondary to economic or other forces (Pal 1992). Despite their growing acceptance, however, studies of institutional arrangements are likely to present a number of research problems because such arrangements can be conceptualised and analysed in many different ways. For example, a structural institutional approach as outlined by Coleman and Skogstad (1990: 2) holds that 'the preferences and values of policy actors are shaped fundamentally by their structural position . . . Political institutions, accordingly, take on a life of their own; as autonomous political actors, they promote certain ideologies and constrain the choices of individuals.' Such an approach examines 'the formal rules, compliance procedures, and standard operating practices' that shape the relationships between individuals in the political system (see Figure 1.2), and the economy (Hall 1986: 19, in Pal 1992: 99). It should also be noted that institutional patterns and processes will vary among and within public policy arenas (see Hawker *et al.* 1979).

Pal (1992) outlines a neo-institutionalist response to the above conceptual and analytical problems. He conceptualises the state-civil society according to three tiers – the state tradition (or macro level), policy sectors (meso level), and policy networks (micro level). The *state tradition* embraces rules and conventions which apply across the full range of state institutions, and which exercise some influence, even modest, on the public policy process. Analysis of a *policy sector* is somewhat foggy as sectoral boundaries are, of course, problematic. Nevertheless, study of *policy networks* within a policy area, for example, should highlight patterns of relationships between state and societal actors and agencies. The following sections take up a number of issues pertaining to each of these three levels.

The institutions of the state

The institutions of modern states may take on a number of forms, roles and responsibilities. The extent of the state's role in tourism varies according to the conditions and circumstances peculiar to each country (politico-economic-constitutional system, socio-economic development, degree of tourism development) (IUOTO 1974: 67). Indeed, IUOTO argued that tourism was such a key sector that in order to foster and develop tourism

> on a scale proportionate to its national importance and to mobilize all available resources to that end, it is necessary to centralize the policy-making powers in the hands of the state so that it can take appropriate measures for creating a suitable framework for the promotion and development of tourism by the various sectors concerned.
>
> (IUOTO 1974: 71)

Tourism is being promoted at all levels of government. For instance, in developed nations such as Canada, the United Kingdom, and the United States, and in less developed countries such as Kenya, Cuba, Sri Lanka (Harrison 1992), tourism development is receiving increasing recognition as a regional, if not national, economic development strategy.

The state is an arena of conflicting values and interests, and there is a need for research to understand which values and interests dominate policy decisions and actions, and what consequences arise from them. Marsh (1983) clearly dismissed the view that the state is a consistent, coherent, cohesive institution, either with a common self-interest, or with a capability of deciding what is best in the national interest. He points out that 'any empirical observation . . . shows that [states] are not undifferentiated wholes, there are more or less important divisions within the executive, and between the executive and the bureaucracy' (Marsh 1983: 12).

Institutional arrangements and the role of the state are significant for tourism. The institutions of the state provide the framework within which tourism operates. Unfortunately, the role of the state has been neglected, although recent studies (e.g. Bramham *et al.* 1989; Urry 1990; Britton 1991; Roche 1992; Hall 1994a) have begun to redress this situation. Nevertheless, good case study material is relatively scarce (Williams and Shaw 1988; Richter 1989; Hall 1991a; Pearce 1992) and limited mainly to the role of government organisations and inter-organisational relations. The majority of studies of tourism policy have been analysis *for* policy rather than analysis *of* policy (e.g. Edgell 1990). In other words, they are prescriptive studies of what government should do rather than examination of what happened and why. Prescriptive studies have some utility, but they yield little insight into the political dimensions of tourism, and certainly lack the potency and impact of studies which raise critical questions concerning whose interests and values are being served by particular policy settings.

Components of institutional arrangements

The notion that institutions are an important factor in tourism public policy implicitly assumes that much behaviour within and outside organisations is rule bound. By rules, March and Olsen (1989: 22) mean 'routines, procedures, conventions, roles, strategies, organisational forms, and technologies around which political activity is constructed . . . [as well as] beliefs, paradigms, codes, cultures, and knowledge that surround, support, elaborate and contradict those roles and routines'. Deciding and acting within a set of rules means considering one's role, the situation (namely, the 'rules of the game'), and deciding on the appropriate decisions and actions. This logic of appropriateness differs from a logic of decision-making concerned only with self-interest (utilitarianism) or one which assumes civil servants act only in the interest of the government of the day. The determination of identity and appropriate action then govern behaviour (Pal 1992).

An institutional approach to tourism public policy processes opens our eyes to the way in which politicians, government departments and authorities, bureaucrats, interest groups, the media and others perceive, understand and act out their roles. Rules or norms, including legislation, government policy platforms, and organisational directives and culture, set boundaries or standards of acceptable behaviour, and these are often imposed upon (as it is difficult for individuals to wilfully ignore them), and then internalised, by actors and agencies (Pal 1992). Therefore, institutional arrangements help shape and structure what people will consider doing. However, these arrangements do not necessarily determine or control action on their own because of personal values, interests and, in the case of bureaucrats, their ability to exercise discretion in the implementation of policy.

Approaches that reduce policy-making to structural factors or assume that individual behaviour is completely rational or self-interested, place little or no emphasis on ideas and meaning (March and Olsen 1989). Institutions, understood, in part, as an intricate web of rules, procedures and roles, require that people think about who they are, and what is appropriate for them to do in terms of a given situation. It should come as no surprise to learn that participants in the policy-making process confront certain ambiguities (e.g. vague policy statements) and are constrained by difficulties of interpreting their roles and responsibilities.

Public policy varies across sectors. If we are looking for institutional patterns, we must remember that they seem to vary by policy sector, and even within sectors. Patterns observed in other public policy arenas (e.g. health or immigration) cannot be assumed to be repeated in the tourism public policy process, nor can we assume that those processes are similar between countries and regions. For example, we can expect tourism policy in the United States to look different from that of South Africa, and policy will be processed, discussed and perceived differently in those countries as well. Therefore, although there may be some similarities, policies and institutional arrangements will differ within and between countries and there may be little integration among tourism organisations.

Different state levels will tend to have different tourism objectives. Study of the tourism public policy process 'is made more complex because the aims of the local state may diverge from those of the central state' (Williams and Shaw 1988: 230). Nowhere may this be more apparent than in federal political systems where there exists three or even four levels of the state: national, state/provincial, regional and local.

> in a federal system, which disperses power among different levels of government, some groups may have more influence if policy is made at the national level; other groups may benefit more if policy is made at the state or provincial level . . . In summary, institutional structures, arrangements, and procedures can have a significant impact on public policy and should not be ignored in policy analysis. Neither should analysis of them, without concern for the dynamic aspects of politics, be considered adequate.
>
> (Anderson 1984: 18)

Tourism public policy is forged and shaped principally within political and public institutions (see Case study 1). For example, this is well recognised in Greece where a draft law 'provided for, among other things, the establishment of new organs and mechanisms, through which the co-operation of the state and the private sector will be institutionalised' (OECD 1992: 71). An understanding of the policy-making process requires a good general knowledge of the machinery of government, and the lines of responsibility, roles and functions of various individuals, bodies and institutions. We might raise concerns as to:

- which individuals and agencies (who) were involved and the nature of their relationships;
- the role of various government and nongovernment agencies;
- the extent of ministerial responsibility in public policy;
- the ability of the bureaucracy to effect or shape public policy in its implementation; and
- how power was exercised 'behind the scenes' by individuals in order to ascertain what pressures were applied and by whom, and what compromises or trade-offs were struck.

Recognition of the institutional arrangements for tourism public policies would provide a conceptual and theoretical approach to investigating many issues of critical importance to tourism public policy. It would take us beyond the analysis of works such as that of Pearce (1992) to contribute to an understanding of what happens in and among organisations and help open the political system ('black box' of decision-making) (see Figure 1.2). Two areas of particular interest in recent tourism studies which are relevant to institutional approaches are inter-governmental relations, and interorganisational and intraorganisational relations.

Case study 1: The restructuring of New Zealand government involvement in tourism

New Zealand has experienced substantial growth in inbound tourism in recent years thanks to a favourable exchange rate, airline deregulation, improved marketing and promotion, and additional international airline capacity. To the year ending October 1994, New Zealand had received 1,291,251 international visitors (New Zealand Tourism Board 1994), a 14 per cent increase over the previous year. The New Zealand Tourism Board (NZTB) (1991) has an ambitious target of attracting three million visitors to New Zealand by the year 2000. A figure which is estimated to have substantial economic benefits including NZ$5.7 billion worth of foreign exchange, but which is also regarded as having potentially negative social, economic and environmental impacts (Chamberlain 1992).

The role of government in New Zealand tourism has changed markedly in recent years. Two government organisations are directly involved in tourism: the NZTB which is responsible for international marketing and promotion, and the Ministry of Tourism which is responsible for policy advice to government. The two organisations were created in 1991, out of the New Zealand Tourism Department (NZTD), which was itself formed in July 1990 from the restructured New Zealand Tourist and Publicity Department (Ministry of Tourism 1991; Pearce 1992). As Chamberlain (1992: 91) observed: 'reforming,

Case study 1 *(continued)*

renaming, structuring, re-logoing and relaunching tourism is an ingrained tradition' in New Zealand. The reorganisation of government involvement in tourism in New Zealand has parallels with the Australian experience where government involvement is primarily being oriented towards marketing and promotion, and the development of infrastructure and product is increasingly left in the hands of the private sector (Hall 1994b, 1995).

In the final corporate plan for the NZTD the Minister of Tourism, John Banks, stated that the creation of the NZTB and the Ministry of Tourism reflected 'the culmination of a direction which has been emerging in previous department plans – the building of an effective relationship with industry in marketing New Zealand as a visitor destination', with the government's overall outcome for tourism being, 'To achieve the highest levels of overseas earnings and employment creation attributable to tourism growth, consistent with the sustainable development of New Zealand as a visitor destination and with maximising the long term benefits to the nation' (NZTD 1991: 2).

The NZTB was established in December 1991, to 'revitalise New Zealand's marketing effort in its international markets' and to 'work closely with the private sector to accelerate the growth of visitor arrivals and increase the length of stay and the amount of money visitors spend in New Zealand' (NZTB 1992). Under the Board's Act, its functions are to 'develop, implement and promote strategies for tourism' and 'advise the government and the New Zealand tourism industry on matters relating to the development, implementation, and promotion of those strategies' (NZTB 1991: 6). The Board's most recently stated mission is 'to ensure that New Zealand is developed and marketed as a competitive tourism destination to maximise the long term benefits to New Zealand' (NZTB 1991: 7).

In response to that mission, the NZTB cut staff in New Zealand in February 1992 from 120 to 75 and boosted overseas staff numbers from 47 to 75 (Vasil 1992). Approximately 80 per cent

Case study 1 *(continued)*

---

of the Board's financial resources are now concentrated on overseas marketing, compared with 60 per cent under the NZTD.
Simultaneously, the number of overseas offices of the NZTB has
been expanded from eight to 14 (Cheyne-Buchanan 1992).

Intergovernmental relations

Governments are constantly taking decisions and actions that affect
tourism. Government is a central institution of the state. Lickorish *et al.*
(1991: 64) identified two roles of government in tourism policy formulation: (1) 'a deliberate action by government introduced to favour
the tourism sector', and (2) any action undertaken 'which may have
implications for tourism, but [which] is not specifically intended to favour
or influence tourism development'. However, in many countries, the
policies and programmes of governments at different levels are poorly
integrated. In short, there is a problem with a lack of coordination as
to tourism policy and action. Policies at one level of government may
contradict policies at another level, or perhaps are implemented with
little consultation between levels.

Intergovernmental relations also transcend national boundaries,
particularly in the areas of international trade and aviation agreements,
customs and immigration. For example, a Joint Australia–New Zealand
Study Team (consisting of staff from the Australian Bureau of Transport
and Communications Economics and Jarden Morgan NZ Limited – now
CS First Boston New Zealand Limited) reported on the *Costs and
Benefits of a Single Australasian Aviation Market*. In raising three single
market scenarios, the report suggested 'that sizeable welfare gains might
be achieved if the Australian and New Zealand aviation markets were
unified under the Closer Economic Relations Agreement' (Australian
Bureau of Transport and Communications Economics and Jarden
Morgan NZ Limited 1991: 32) between Australia and New Zealand.
Governments may also undertake complementary research, marketing
and promotional efforts. The World Tourism Organisation, for instance,
provides 'a world clearinghouse for the collection, analysis, and dissemination of technical tourism information. It offers national tourism
administrations and organisations the machinery for a multinational

approach to international discussions and negotiations on important tourism matters' (Edgell 1990: 46).

Interorganisational relations

Interorganisational relations among tourist organisations have only recently attracted the attention of academics and practitioners. This is a curious situation. As Selin and Beason (1991: 643) observe, many interdependencies underlie interactions among tourism organisations. From its long chain of distribution systems to its fragmented supply components (see the discussion on the partial industrialisation of tourism in Chapter 4), the tourism field is, by its very nature, dependent upon interorganisational relations to achieve organisational and regional goals. Interorganisational relations can be upon mutually agreed terms, cooperative and beneficial to organisations as they seek self-interests. The notion of self-interest also tells us, however, that interorganisational relations need not always be cooperative and mutually supportive. Organisations also interact as they compete for resources and seek different policy outcomes (Warren et al. 1974).

An interorganisational relationship exists when two or more organisations interact and trade resources with each other. These resources may comprise financial, technical or human resources and include customer or client referrals (Selin and Beason 1991; Pearce 1992). An interorganisational relationship may be very temporary, it may be irregular (developed and terminated according to need), or it may be long term. The nature of this relationship and the behaviour of organisations within it can be examined in a number of ways. However, two main approaches to studying this interaction have emerged (Pearce 1992). The first is one based on exchange theory as presented in the seminal paper by Levine and White (1961, in Pearce 1992), where organisations are seen to interact voluntarily (perhaps forming policy coalitions) to achieve mutual organisational goals. The second approach stresses power or resource dependency (Pfeffer and Salancik 1978, in Selin and Beason 1991; Pearce 1992) and treats the interorganisational network as a political economy so that organisations are seen to be induced to interact by a more powerful organisation (or collection of organisations).

Issues arising from interorganisational studies are numerous. Some of the more common features observed in the tourism field (Selin and Beason 1991; Pearce 1992) include:

- resource acquisition (namely, financial, human resources, technical knowledge, and authority);
- coordination through legal mandates or otherwise; and
- resource scarcity and conflict.

To study interorganisational relationships, students of tourism must, among other things, identify and access the relevant key actors and agencies, examine the values, perceptions, and interests of significant individuals and organisations, and isolate the relationships within and between stakeholders in the tourism policy process.

Summary

The approach described in this chapter assumes that an important, perhaps first, step in gaining a realistic understanding of tourism public policy is to take institutional arrangements seriously. In doing so, institutions must be understood as more than the state writ large (Pal 1992). The analysis of institutions can have as its subject the rules at many levels of decision-making, and therefore such analysis should not be confined to a single level. Nevertheless, it is clearly important that researchers keep the distinction between levels firmly in mind if cogent analyses and meaningful policy advice and prescriptions are to result.

By disaggregating the state, it might be possible to see where the effects of macro-structures are most prominent in the tourism public policy process, and to observe why and how different sectors vary in the way in which tourism public policy is processed. It might even be possible to argue that some areas of policy require certain types of policy process in order to function efficiently (Pal 1992). International and national effectiveness in tourism policy-making may require highly coordinated policy networks so that planning and effective implementation are possible. Pluralism in these sectors may in fact waste valuable time and resources as private and state actors fail to agree on priorities and plans so that inaction and non-decisions pervade the policy process.

Questions for review and discussion

1 Discuss the importance of institutional arrangements for tourism policy studies.
2 Why is it important to conceptualise and analyse the institutional arrangements for tourism at three levels?

3 Why might the institutional arrangements for tourism be seen to have different forms, roles and responsibilities in different countries?
4 What are the two main approaches to studying interorganisational relations in tourism? How do these approaches differ? What are the implications of each approach in terms of their understanding of interorganisational relations?

Guide to further reading

For general discussions of the nature and study of institutional arrangements in modern states, readers should consult: Simeon (1976); Ostrom 1986; Dye (1992); Pal (1992); Brooks (1993); March and Olsen (1989) and Coleman and Skogstad (1990).

More tourism-specific discussions relating to institutional arrangements, or aspects of those arrangements, are referred to in Williams and Shaw (1988); Richter (1989); Edgell (1990); Selin and Beason (1991); Pearce (1992); and Roche (1992).

3
Values in the tourism policy-making process

When the goals of policies are not questioned because they are the values which must be kept separate from facts, the analyst becomes committed to the value context of those policies, even if his political ideology would not support them if he looked more carefully at them . . . There is neither politics nor political science left when we can look at Eichmann and ask only whether his policymaking system was as good as it might have been.

(Lowi 1970: 319)

The role of values in tourism policy

Values lie at the core of public policy and, hence, of tourism policy. For example, in the case of environmental policy-making, Henning (1974: 15) observed that 'decisions affecting environmental policies grow out of a political process. This process involves the *values* of individuals, groups and organizations in the struggle for *power* through human interaction relative to the decision.' Lindblom (1959: 82) stated that 'one chooses among values and among policies at one and the same time', and that 'the administrator focuses his attention on marginal or incremental values'. Similarly, Simmons *et al.* (1974: 457) noted that 'it is value choice, implicit and explicit, which orders the priorities of government and determines the commitment of resources within the public jurisdiction'.

Although values are central to an understanding of the tourism policy-making process we should note that much social science research, including much tourism research, often ignores this situation and treats facts and values as separate entities. However, we argue that this situation is simply unrealistic if one is seeking to understand how the policy process operates and what the outcomes and impacts of the process represent to the people who are affected by government decisions.

Public policies are therefore representative of value choices. For example, to declare an area a wilderness park rather than allow mining to occur may represent the dominance of environmental values over economic values. Value and value change therefore lie at the heart of our understanding of tourism and public policy. The impacts of values on public policies occur at numerous levels of analysis and throughout the policy process. We can talk of the importance of macro-level sets of values or ideologies which operate at the national level, e.g. in terms of the old Cold War dichotomy of capitalism and communism. We can also note the impact of ideology and political philosophy on government policies and actions. For instance, in the change of government priorities for tourism that may occur when a conservative government is replaced by a liberal or democratic socialist government.

Values also play a role within and between organisations. The term 'organisational culture' refers, in part, to a shared set of values, norms and procedures that operate within organisations. For example, to express this in its most simple form it can be argued that national park agencies are more geared towards conservation and visitation than forestry agencies which are more concerned with timber yields. Although the agencies may be responsible for similar natural resources their management and planning approaches to those resources are fundamentally different because of their agency objectives and associated organisational cultures.

Individual values are also significant in the policy-making process. Individual decisions and actions are a reflection of personal and organisational values. Individuals also get involved in the political process through, for example, membership of political parties and interest groups, in order to try to affect public policy. Individual and collective cultural values are also important, for example, in the representation of heritage to tourists and in conflicts over the authenticity and validity of tourist and heritage experiences.

Values therefore underlie all tourism policy. Many values often appear hidden, perhaps because we take them so much for granted and tend to ignore their research and applied implications. If we are to understand tourism public policy, it is vital that we shed light on the values that tourism policies represent, and on the winners and losers in the policy-making process.

Values and ideology

Values are 'ends, goals, interests, beliefs, ethics, biases, attitudes, traditions, morals and objectives that change with human perception and with time, and that have a significant influence on power conflicts relating to policy' (Henning 1974: 15). The concept of values is closely related to that of ideology. An ideology is a system of belief about some important social area or issue that has strong effects in structuring and influencing our thought. While some ideologies grow from a consensus or a tradition, others have been constructed by philosophers or by the media (Brown 1973). As with policies, ideologies may be represented in a constitution, a declaration of rights, a treatise, or from communications that are designed to influence behaviours, attitudes and values. As with values, we are often not aware of the ideologies that exist within our own society. For example, in Western society tourism and leisure are something to be 'consumed', selected from an array of offerings produced and distributed by a highly competitive and enterprising tourism industry (Britton 1991; Hall 1994a). This ideology, and the dynamism and volatility of the leisure and tourism market, helps perpetuate the notion that 'fun' and 'entertainment' are entirely free of political consequences. As Wilson (1988: 52) recognised, 'the ideology of "consumer sovereignty" encourages us to regard leisure choice as an exercise in individual freedom; and it lends support to the notion that politics, which connote domination and control, should be kept out of leisure'.

Ideologies are therefore extremely important in legitimising, defining and identifying particular attitudes, whether positive or negative, and interests in social and political issues. Indeed, Craik (1990: 43) in commenting on the formulation of tourism policy argued that 'governments and communities need to reconsider the *ideological* basis of public policy that currently endorses *values* of economic rationalism, free market play, user pays, de-regulation, and so on'.

One needs to differentiate between state (macro), organisational (meso) and individual (micro) ideologies. Many people hold systems of attitudes, beliefs and values that can rightly be termed ideologies. As

Brown (1973: 12) recognised, 'since the members of any society will have ideas, beliefs and opinions about their society's organization and values, norms of honesty and goodness, freedom and equality belong themselves to an integrated ideology' (also see Rokeach 1973).

Values and governance

Within Western society considerable debate has emerged in the past two decades over the appropriate role of the state in society (see Chapter 2). Throughout most of the 1980s the rise of 'Thatcherism' (named after Conservative Prime Minister Margaret Thatcher) in the United Kingdom and 'Reaganism' (named after Republican President Ronald Reagan) in the United States saw a period of retreat by central governments from active government intervention. At the national level, policies of deregulation, privatisation, the elimination of tax incentives, and a move away from discretionary forms of macro-economic intervention, were the hallmarks of a push towards 'smaller' government and the supposed withdrawal of government from the economy.

Tourism is not immune from such changes in political philosophy. Tourism is subject to direct and indirect government intervention primarily because of its employment and income producing possibilities. Given calls for smaller government in Western society in recent years, there have been increasing demands from conservative national governments and economic rationalists for greater industry self-sufficiency in tourism marketing and promotion, often through the privatisation or corporatisation of tourism agencies or boards (Jeffries 1989). The implications of such an approach for the tourism industry are substantial. As Hughes (1984: 14) noted, 'The advocates of a free enterprise economy would look to consumer freedom of choice and not to governments to promote firms; the consumer ought to be sovereign in decisions relating to the allocation of the nation's resources.'

Privatisation of tourism agencies would mean that the tourist industry would have to pay for regional and national promotion itself rather than rely on public funding. For example, the draft report of the Industries Assistance Commission (IAC) Inquiry into Travel and Tourism (1989a) in Australia recommended that government funding for the Australian Tourist Commission, the federally funded national tourism promotion body, be phased out over five years and national promotion be taken over by the private sector (Craik 1990) (see

Chapter 4). However, this did not happen as the tourism industry lobby groups were able to convince both the Commission and the Australian government that tourism promotion would not be adequately funded by industry alone.

Institutional arrangements are a reflection of broader values in the political process. Over the past 15 years tourism organisations have tended to take on a more commercial outlook. Within times of recession, tourist organisations are primarily geared more towards maximising visitor numbers and economic benefits than to the social and environmental effects of tourism. In addition, the move towards smaller, more 'business-like' government has often meant that tourism organisations tend to be managed more like private sector organisations (e.g. boards of directors or advisory boards comprised of members of the tourism industry), than government departments with a broader sense of public service and public good.

Despite the reduced role of national governments in economic intervention, the local state has increased its involvement in economic activity. The local state comprises 'local authorities as well as the local/regional representatives of various national-level bodies, including tourist boards' (Urry 1990: 112). Regional (e.g. provincial or state) and local government has traditionally had a role in economic development. However, the present economic activity of the local state is qualitatively different from that which has existed in the past. Reduced central government funding, economic recession, and a changing global economy have increased the pressures on the local state to create employment opportunities, and to attract investment and income generating industries. Indeed, it is perhaps ironic that the reduced role of central government in positive economic development strategies was a major factor in the creation of the new economic roles for the local state.

Eisinger (1988) has described this new style of interventionist local state as 'the entrepreneurial state'. Here the local state, typically in partnership with the private sector, becomes an active player in the market through the adoption of a variety of policy instruments. The traditional economic development strategies of the local state concentrated on such supply-side factors as incentives that lowered costs (capital, land and labour), including loans, loan guarantees, tax exemptions and lower tax rates. The new entrepreneurial state increasingly focuses on demand-side strategies which aim to discover, develop, expand and create new markets.

Tourism and leisure are an essential part of the economic development strategies of the local state. The creation of urban development corporations and enterprise boards is tied in with urban and regional redevelopment programmes seeking to 'rejuvenate' inner-city and industrial lands. Urban revitalisation typically includes the development of inner-city leisure spaces, waterfront redevelopments, festival marketplaces, casinos, conference centres and sports stadia. In this urban environment, the creation of leisure spaces is both a mechanism to attract tourists and new investment. The city becomes a product to be bought and sold. Therefore, cities and regions in the new entrepreneurial local state constantly seek to image and reimage themselves in order to promote themselves as attractive places to live, work, invest and play.

Urban space is therefore reconstructed in a manner which meets the imaging needs of demand-side economic development strategies. The hosting of large-scale sporting and cultural events, dockland redevelopment projects, the creation of heritage precincts, downtown revitalisation schemes, the opening or refurbishment of museums and art galleries, and the establishment of city cultural policies are all components of reimaging. As Urry (1990: 119) observed: 'In recent years almost every town and city in Britain has been producing mixed development waterfront schemes in which tourist appeal is one element.' However, according to Mommaas and van der Poel (1989: 263) the development of a more economically oriented city development policy style, aimed at the revitalisation of the city, has led to 'projects, developed in public–private partnerships, [which] are meant not for the integration of disadvantaged groups within society, but for servicing the pleasures of the well-to-do'.

Tourism has a problematic role within the local state. As is often the case, the perception by local and regional governments is that tourism is a ready source of employment opportunities and will be an income generator. However, the change of values in attitudes towards tourism has meant that the bigger picture of tourism within economic and social development processes is often being lost. It may be argued that the present situation is representative of a crisis of the local state in Western societies in which traditional social welfare concerns have been replaced by entrepreneurial concerns in which city centres are gaining resources at the expense of the interests of those in the suburbs (Henry and Bramham 1986; Hall 1994a).

Case study 2: Atlantic City

Atlantic City has a long history as a tourist destination. At the turn of the century, Atlantic City was probably the most famous resort in the United States. In the summer of 1925, the city had over 1,000 hotels and 21 theatres. However, after the Second World War, the tourist trade entered a period of substantial decline as tourists increasingly travelled to Florida.

By the mid-1970s unemployment levels in Atlantic City had reached 13 per cent and the Central Business District had suffered a 12 per cent decline in employment since 1972. The population of 40,000 had no supermarket, no theatre and only one cinema (which showed 'adult' movies!). In response, the city leadership sought to legalise gambling in the city in order to increase tourism, economic development, and city and state revenues. A state referendum was passed, and in 1978, Resorts International opened the first casino.

By the late 1980s, the city had more than US$6 million in assessed property making it the richest city in the United States in terms of assessed property value per capita, and it was the most popular American tourist destination. The casinos also created 48,000 new jobs, more than the city's population. A focus on tourist, tax base and employment figures would suggest that the economic development strategy of legalising gambling and encouraging casino development was an outstanding success. Few, if any, other cities which have suffered economic decline have recorded a 21-fold increase in their property tax base in 14 years.

However, there is another side to this economic success story. Between 1977 and 1982, 20 per cent of the city's housing stock was demolished to make way for casino development. The local economy became less diversified and more dependent on the tourist industry, while the manufacturing sector underwent rapid decline as land values increased. The benefits of casino development have been unevenly distributed. The surrounding suburbs, such as Galloway and Egg Harbour, have gained far more economically as many of the casino workers live outside of the central city. The anticipated 'multiplier effect' in the central

Case study 2 *(continued)*

---

city did not occur. 'Many local residents are still poor and unemployed, half of the population still receives public assistance, and city services still continue to be substandard. Social problems, including increased crime and prostitution, are worse than ever' (Teske and Sur 1991: 130).

Source: Steinlieb and Hughes 1983; Dombrink and Thompson 1990; Teske and Sur 1991.

The changing uses of tourism in former state socialist nations

Given the massive political and economic changes that have been wrought in the former state socialist countries of Eastern Europe, it should not be surprising that tourism is perceived as a major component of economic restructuring in those countries. Tourism is regarded as an economic escape route for the former state socialist countries of Eastern Europe and East Asia, and for many less developed nations. As Hall (1991b: 4) argued, 'the relatively labour-intensive nature of the tourism industry, and the limited scope for capital substitution in the production of tourism services may be particularly compelling for these societies which are experiencing, for the first time in a half a century, significant and increasing unemployment problems'.

The economic changes which are occurring with respect to tourism in Eastern Europe are matched by major political changes in which the values attached to tourism have undergone substantial revision. In the former state socialist nations, tourism played an important ideological function for the state in promoting model communist behaviour and activity (Hall 1991a; Hall 1994a). The role of tourism in the former German Democratic Republic (East Germany) was typical of the Eastern European situation. For instance, there was 'considerable emphasis on group recreation and holidays in accommodation provided by the workplace or trade union ... designed to build social coherence and an esprit-de-corps, besides allowing recreation time to be mixed with political indoctrination' (Mellor 1991: 149). However, leisure travel in Eastern Europe is now being driven by the necessities of economic development, and the expression of new foreign policies, political identities, and values. In the case of Hungary

> The downgrading of tourism from the countries that comprised Communist Eastern Europe until late 1989 has been deliberate as Hungary has positively sought to attract visitors from the West by relaxing bureaucratic and monetary constraints. Initially, the motive was the country's desperate need for hard currency, but it is now part of the process of political liberalisation and an assertion of Hungary's independence.
>
> (Compton 1991: 188)

Tourism still plays an important ideological function in Eastern Europe even if it is not as overt as during the period of state socialism. The decline of state socialism has led to a revival of cultural practices and traditions which had been curtailed under the former regimes. Heritage tourism, in particular, has become especially important in the forging of post-communist national and cultural identities. 'The immediate past state-socialist period has quickly become the source of a new heritage industry' (Hall 1991c: 284). The relics of the communist period have become relegated to the backs of museums or have become political tourist curiosities. Tourists can now visit political prisons to experience the communist past, while also seeing churches and heritage sites which have been closed to visitors for many years. History is being re-written and re-presented in order both to attract foreign tourists and to forge new national identities and political values by reference to a pre-communist past.

In both East and West, therefore, the economic and political functions of tourism are representative of political value systems. In the former state socialist countries of Eastern Europe these values were often extremely overt. Nevertheless, it is important to emphasise that tourism is also utilised by Western countries to achieve political objectives. For example, there are no direct flights between the United States and Cuba because of American trade restrictions on that country. Furthermore, the manner in which heritage is represented to the visitor may be of critical importance in conveying certain values to the tourist to the exclusion of other values (see Chapter 5). However, as the next sections highlight, values are not only significant at the government or state level, but are also important at the organisational and community level.

Values at the organisational level

The organisational dimension of tourism has been little studied. With the exception of the valuable contribution of Pearce (1992) and annual OECD reports, the organisational component of tourism has been a by-product rather than a focus of research. The previous chapter indicated the importance of organisations as part of the framework of institutional arrangements for tourism policy-making. However, tourism organisations also have a substantial value component which, with few exceptions (e.g. Craik 1990), is ignored in the tourism literature.

Tourism organisations act both as a filter and as a source of tourism policy. Traditionally, government bureaucracies have been represented as value-neutral whereby they simply follow government objectives with the utmost economy and efficiency. However, such a notion of bureaucratic activity is defunct. Bureaucrats are not immune to political struggles and, hence, value competition. As Albrow (1970: 22) observed, 'Where everything is done through a bureaucracy, nothing to which a bureaucracy is really averse can be done at all.' Bureaucratic bodies cannot be neutral instruments; inevitably they develop powers and styles of behaviour that press in certain directions, and close off potential policy pathways. It is impossible for bureaucracies to be value-neutral because, as organisations, their structure, objectives and activities are representative of some values to the exclusion of others.

Organisational structure will exert a strong influence on organisational values and culture. Indeed, it can be argued that the shift towards more corporate models in government economic strategies discussed above will be reflected in a similar shift in tourism organisational values. For instance, in Australia and New Zealand there have been wholesale changes in government involvement in tourism whereby promotion and marketing concerns have been emphasised at the expense of planning and development concerns (Hall 1995). This has corresponded with substantial job losses in the planning sections of tourism agencies and position gains in the marketing area. Policy, planning and development branches of government agencies have been minimised in size while the promotional dimensions of tourist organisations have been maximised. The government focus is therefore on tourism numbers rather than the net benefits that tourism can bring to a destination. In this setting, important issues surrounding the supply of tourism product and infrastructure are likely to be ignored by government and left to market solutions.

Tourism organisations which are wholly government controlled will have different sets of corporate values than agencies which have a degree of statutory independence and which are closely linked to the private sector orientation of the tourism industry. One of the fundamental differences is the provision for the direct influence of non-departmental people acting as Commissioners, or in effect a board of directors. 'The implications of a Board of Directors linked to private industry, within the confines of a QUANGO (Quasi Autonomous Government Organisation), are that perhaps the balance of power swings to private developers' (Jenkins 1993a: 284) who will have a more commercial orientation towards tourism. For example, Simon Baggs, the Director of Marketing with the New South Wales Tourism Commission, described the organisation as primarily a marketing organisation, in spite of the fact the front page of the Commission's *1990/91 Annual Report* clearly stated that the agency has the task of 'maximising the economic, social and cultural benefits of tourism for the people of New South Wales' (1991: 1). 'There was a lot of blood on the carpet, we abolished 30 jobs. In a way that will fund the Sydney push. That's the painful side, but its reality. We're not at all protected from the real world' (Simon Baggs, quoted in Burbury 1991).

Organisational values do undergo generational change, and new governments or new ways of thinking about public policy and public administration do influence government organisational attitudes and functions. Nevertheless, it is important to stress that the development of organisational values will tend to be more one of continuity than change. Individuals are often fired and hired according to the ethos and objectives of an organisation, thereby providing for the reinforcement of the existing organisational culture. Organisational pressures to conform are created through general socialisation, the recruitment and training of staff, and the development or severing of community networks that are part of professionalisation. Students of tourism policy and planning therefore need to recognise the nature of organisational values and culture if emphasis is being placed on policy change and reform. The prospects of the successful implementation of new tourism policies will be related to the receptivity, structure and values of tourist organisations.

Values at the individual and community level

All individuals have values which serve as the basis for political decision-making. Individual and collective values provide the foundation for the policy arena in which tourism policy-making occurs. Tourism policy-making is an arena of competing and complementary values and interests. Often these values are articulated by organised groups (see Chapter 5). At other times the values of significant individual actors, such as senior politicians, bureaucrats, or industry figures, will influence the path that a policy takes in its formulation and implementation.

Much of the interest in values in tourism has been focused on issues of value change arising from the influence of tourism. The role that tourism can play in transforming collective and individual values is inherent in ideas of commoditisation (Cohen 1977) which states that personal 'cultural displays' of 'authentic' contemporary traditions become a 'cultural product' which meets tourists' needs. 'We no longer discuss [the arts] as expressions of imagination or creativity, we talk about "product"; we are no longer moved by the experiences the arts have to offer, we "consume" them. Culture has become a commodity' (Hewison 1988: 240).

The value change associated with tourism does not just occur through the transformation of socio-cultural activities into products. In a comparative study of two Austrian Alpine villages, Vent and Obergurgl, changes in the value orientations of each village community appeared to be strongly related to the economic structural changes initiated by tourism (Meleghy et al. 1985). In this situation, it was also noted that the value change induced by tourism influenced community political structures. Undoubtedly, the introduction of other new forms of economic activity would also probably have certain value and structural effects. Tourism is often blamed for every value transformation under the sun (Crick 1989). Nevertheless, the service nature of the tourism industry, with a high level of personal contact between the product and the purchaser, may well create processes of acculturation and value change which are peculiar to tourism (Hall 1994a).

Heritage is one area of tourism in which value change and value conflict within communities is receiving more attention from government, industry and academics. By its very definition, heritage – the things we want to keep – is concerned with the preservation and representation of values. Heritage is therefore a flexible concept which indicates selective reinterpretations of the past. The history which is part of the fund of knowledge of a community is not necessarily what has actually been preserved by popular memory, but what has been selected, written, pictured, popularised and institutionalised by those with the power to do so (see Chapter 5). Within the context of tourism development, communities reconstruct the past and reinterpret the present. Particular ideologies represent themselves to the gaze of the tourist through museums, historic houses, historic monuments, guided tours, public spaces, heritage precincts, and tourist landscapes. The gaze of the tourist is not value-neutral, and the representation of heritage may act to legitimate contemporary social and political structures. As Norkunas (1993: 5) recognised, 'The public would accept as "true" history that is written, exhibited, or otherwise publicly sanctioned. What is often less obvious to the public is that the writing or the exhibition itself is reflective of a particular ideology.'

Visitors are often unaware of the contested nature of history and do not ask the question: whose interpretation of history are we seeing? However, in recent years the presentation of heritage to tourists is becoming increasingly contested. For example, native peoples are seeking a greater say in how their history is presented to visitors. Similarly, the decision by the Walt Disney Company not to proceed with its plans for an historical theme park at Manassas, Virginia, site of the Bull Run United States Civil War battle, was as much opposed on cultural concerns as it was on environmental grounds. 'A broad coalition of historians, politicians and pundits argued that the project would trivialise the country's history, and insisted that Mickey Mouse had no place in such momentous events as the abolition of slavery or the carnage of the Civil War' (Macintyre 1994: 16).

The contestation of the past between different groups and individuals in a community is indicative of the broader pattern of tourism policy-making. Value conflict is entrenched in tourism policy-making. As the next chapter indicates, different interests, with different sets of values, compete with each other to influence or control the tourism policy agenda. The success of these groups is relative to their power within the policy arena, an issue which is dealt with in more detail in Chapter 5.

Summary

Values lie at the heart of tourism policy-making. This chapter began with a discussion of the nature of values and their relationship to ideology. Values are the overarching criteria people use to make decisions. An ideology is a systematic representation of those values. The implications of values for tourism was then discussed in relation to the three levels of analysis. First, at the level of the state, where the changing role of government in tourism was related to broader political value change. Second, at the level of the organisation values were seen to act as a 'filter' in the tourism policy process. In addition, they were considered to have a life of their own in terms of their contribution to the development of an 'organisational culture'. Finally, this chapter discussed values at the individual and community level. It was argued that tourism both creates and responds to value change, and that the value-laden nature of tourism is becoming increasingly recognised and contested, particularly within the cultural and heritage aspects of tourism development.

Questions for review and discussion

1 How have changes in political values affected the role of tourism in government?
2 What relationship, if any, exists between institutional arrangements and values in tourism policy-making?
3 How can heritage preservation be said to represent the dominance of one set of values over another?
4 Is it possible to reconcile environmental and economic values in tourism?

Guide to further reading

Most public policy and public administration texts will contain a discussion of the role of values in the policy-making process. Of particular interest is Simmons and Dvorin (1977).

For a useful discussion of the changing role of tourism in contemporary government and its relationship to broader political values see Hall (1991a), Williams and Shaw (1988) and Hall (1994a). For case studies at the micro-level refer to Meleghy *et al.* (1985) and Roche (1992). For an excellent study on the relationship between values and cultural representation see Hollinshead (1992).

4
The role of interest groups in the tourism policy process

Politics is not attractive, even as a spectator sport, to the majority of people. Organized group politics is even less attractive.

(Zeigler 1980: 11)

The role of interest groups in tourism policy

Government is the focus of demands articulated through a variety of structures and channels including significant individuals, institutions, and the media. Indeed, many groups are formed especially to articulate political demands.

Interests represent the goals that actors (individual or group) seek to achieve in the policy-making process. Because there are different sets of interests working to influence policy formulation and implementation, competition and conflict may occur. Individuals can only assert a certain degree of influence on the policy-making process, therefore blocs of interests or 'interest groups' are a major component in the determination of policy settings.

Since the Second World War there has been a tremendous expansion in the number and scope of interest groups in the policy-making process (Cigler and Loomis 1986). Up until the 1960s, interest groups were primarily business-association based. However, since the early 1960s, there has been rapid growth in Western nations in the number of citizen and public interest groups, particularly in the area of consumer and environmental concerns (Schlozman and Tierney 1986). In addition, individual corporations and business organisations also engage in lobbying. For example, in the United States the number of corporations with offices in Washington increased tenfold between 1961 and 1982 (Colgate 1982).

Tourism policy-making has not been immune from the growth in interest groups. Until the mid-1960s, tourism-related interest groups were generally confined to industry and professional associations. However, the growth of consumer and environmental organisations extended the number of groups who had an interest in tourism issues, particularly as they related to aspects of tourism development at the local level. In the 1980s and the early 1990s, the range of groups was extended still further as social issues, often in relation to developing countries, and international trade became significant and, in terms of the latter, more pervasive. Therefore, it is important to realise that tourism interest groups go well beyond those which are part of the tourism industry and include a vast array of community, public and special interest groups.

Interest groups are an integral component of the tourism policy-making process, and of institutional arrangements in general. However, the expansion of interest groups and therefore of the range of demands placed on government, makes it increasingly difficult for government to satisfy those demands to the extent where some commentators have referred to government overload. According to Cigler (1991: 101) 'the heightened visibility of groups in the policy and electoral processes, appeared to parallel the diminished capacity of the government to deal with economic and social problems'. Indeed, in an earlier article, he had argued that the proliferation of special interest groups lies at the heart of the problems of contemporary governance and policy-making. In particular, the question of 'how to formulate solutions for complex policy questions in an environment characterized by numerous diverse interests – many passionately expressed – yet with few means to aggregate them' (Cigler 1985: 319).

The following chapter outlines the nature of the interest group concept and details the crowded and highly complex policy-making environment within which tourism-related interest groups operate. Special emphasis is given to the relationship between business and government and the extent to which the tourism industry may influence tourism policy. The final section highlights the fine balance that exists between interest group consultation and incorporation in the policy-making process.

The interest group concept

The term 'interest group' tends to be used interchangeably with the terms 'pressure group', 'lobby group', 'special interest group' or 'organised interests'. For the purpose of this book, an interest group is defined as any association or organisation which makes a claim, either directly or indirectly, on government so as to influence public policy without itself being willing to exercise the formal powers of government (Matthews 1980). Several features of interest groups can be observed:

- Interest groups, while attempting to influence governments, do not seek to gain government. The attempt to win government is the role of political parties. Even if an interest group runs a single issue candidate in an election this should be seen as an attempt to gain further publicity for the group's cause rather than an attempt to gain government.
- Not all activities of an interest group need be political.
- Interest groups will often seek to influence government policy indirectly by attempting to shape the demands that other groups and the general public make on government, e.g. through the conduct of public relations campaigns.
- The term 'interest group' is often cast in a negative light by politicians. However, it must be emphasised that the expression is used by public policy analysts in a value-neutral way to refer to groups that attempt to influence public policy.

Interest groups operate at a number of different scales, e.g. international, national, regional and local. However, interest groups can also be classified along a continuum, according to their degree of institutionalisation, as producer groups, non-producer groups and single interest groups (Matthews 1976). Producer groups, such as business organisations, labour organisations and professional associations, tend to have a high level of organisational resources, a stable membership maintained by the ability of the group to provide benefits to members, ability to gain access to government, and a high level of credibility in bargaining and negotiations with government and other interest groups. In non-producer groups, institutionalisation has occurred on the basis of a common interest of continuing relevance to members, e.g. organisations such as consumer and environmental groups. Single-interest groups are at the other end of the continuum from producer groups and are characterised by their limited degree of organisational permanence, as they will likely disappear altogether once their interests have been achieved or have been rendered unattainable. Table 4.1 illustrates the various types of institutionalised interest groups that occur at different scales in the tourism policy-making process.

Table 4.1 Tourism interest groups

Scale	Producer groups	Non-producer groups	Single-interest groups
International	World Travel & Tourism Council	Environmental and social organisations, e.g. Tourism Concern, International Union for the Conservation of Nature and Natural Resources (IUCN), World Wildlife Fund	Occasional environmental or social issues. often location specific, e.g. campaign to End Child Prostitution in Asian Tourism (ECPAT), or campaign to end golf course development in South-East Asia
National	National tourism industry associations, trade unions, national professional and trade associations	Environmental and consumer organisations, e.g. National Trust, the Wilderness Society, Sierra Club	Single-issue environmental groups, e.g. those opposing airport development
Local	Chambers of Commerce, regional tourism business associations	Rate-payers and resident associations	Groups opposed to tourist development in a specific location, e.g. anti-resort development groups, Olympic Bread and Circus coalitions

The categorisation of interest groups can be extremely useful in understanding their resources, methods and effectiveness in the policy-making process. The continuing relevance of group objectives to their members and the corresponding degree of organisational permanence, will clearly influence the resource base of groups and their continued visibility. For example, the Sierra Club in the United States grew from a small, local, hiking and nature appreciation society in the late nineteenth century and a regionally based nature preservation group in the early twentieth society, to what is presently probably the most influential conservation organisation in the nation, with concerns covering the full range of environmental issues (Cohen 1988).

The complexity of interest group influence

Tourism is a highly crowded and complex policy environment. Leiper's (1989) concept of partial industrialisation helps explain why tourism policy-making can be so complex. Partial industrialisation refers to a situation in which

only certain organisations providing goods and services directly to tourists are in the tourism industry. The proportion of (a) goods and services stemming from that industry to (b) total goods and services used by tourists can be termed the index of industrialisation, theoretically ranging from 100% (wholly industrialised) to zero (tourists present and spending money, but no tourism industry).

(Leiper 1989: 25)

Confusion over the nature of tourism therefore contributes to uncertainty surrounding which groups have a legitimate contribution to make to tourism policy. Although we can recognise that many segments of the economy benefit from tourism, it is only those organisations with a direct relationship to tourists that may become actively involved in tourism policy-making. The diffuse nature of the tourism industry may well mean that even the groups which directly benefit from tourists will have different policy objectives. For example, airlines will tend to seek to carry as many people as possible in a short space of time, whereas the accommodation sector will also aim to reach their capacity but will encourage people to stay as long as possible. The different economic objectives of the two sectors will therefore place different sets of demands on tourism policy and the actions of government tourism agencies, particularly with respect to promotion and marketing strategies. However, tourism policy-making is not just affected by a narrow band of interests. As the following sections indicate, there remains a wide array of groups that seek to have their goals satisfied in the policy-making process.

Business as an interest group

One of the key issues in understanding the tourism policy process is identifying the role of business interests in determining policy. Despite the growth of public interest, consumer, environmental and community-based organisations in the last two decades, Schlozman (1984: 1029) argued that 'the pressure system is tilted heavily in favor of the well-off, especially business'. The perception that business dominates policy-making has been a major concern for students of the policy process over the years. One of the strongest accounts of the business–government relationship comes from American political scientist Charles Lindblom.

Lindblom (1977) argued that in all private enterprise market-oriented societies, business occupies a privileged position in the public policy process. Business performance affects employment, prices, inflation, production, growth and the material standard of living, which are items utilised by government at all levels to measure success. Therefore, government leadership may well be strongly influenced by business leadership in order to achieve certain public policy goals. Indeed, Craik (1990: 29) observed that 'the private sector claims that because it takes risks, it should shape policy'. Nevertheless, as she went on to note, 'the fostering of the private sector by government inevitably leads to charges of clientelism, the coincidence between policy outcomes and the interests of key lobbyists'.

According to Lindblom (1977) a common tacit understanding exists between business and government in Western economies in terms of the general conditions necessary for profitable private enterprise operations. Conflict between business and government typically lies within a small range, which does not touch the primary principles of private enterprise, private property in productive assets, and a substantial measure of business autonomy. Disputes are usually confined to secondary issues such as industrial relations, environmental and social impacts, and, particularly in the case of tourism, the appropriate level of taxation and government support for promotion and infrastructure.

Lindblom argued that business not only controls the agenda but also engages in interest group activity to supplement its privileged position. On those secondary issues that are contested by others, such as trade unions and environmental groups, business interest group activity is regarded as being much more effective than that of its rivals in the public policy-making process. Business wins proportionately in policy debates with other interest groups because, while other interests compete using their members' own incomes and energies, business is able to use corporate resources, thereby giving business a triple advantage – in funds, organisation and access. The size of industry lobbying is substantial. The size of industry influence is substantial. For example, in the case of the United States, Airey (1984: 271) noted that 'most airlines, hotel companies and bus operators etc maintain full-time Washington DC representation. In addition, in 1981, 22 travel-related trade associations had headquarters in the capital. Seven had Washington-based govern-ment relations offices, and 11 were represented there by law or public relations firms.'

Affiliation in general business associations and trade associations amplifies the organised voice of business. Lindblom believed that business's privileged position is widely accepted because business has shaped citizens' beliefs through workplace socialisation and ownership of the media. Primary issues are not raised because the people have been persuaded that the issues are discouragingly complex, not worth their energy, or that agitation is bad or unlikely to succeed.

Although it is clear that business has a major influence on tourism policy, it should be noted that business does not always speak with a unified voice. Given the coordination problems posed by the partial industrialisation of the tourism industry noted above, tourism businesses may well be in disagreement over policy positions. For example, a nature-based tourism operation may well be in support of declaring an area a national park with a low degree of visitor access, whereas a mass tourist business operation may prefer the area being developed as a golf course or theme park with high visitor access. Furthermore, there may be differences in objectives between tourism corporations and organisations in different industry sectors and different industry representative organ-isations, while conflict between business organisations may also occur on an inter-regional scale.

In order to meet the wishes of its members, peak tourism industry bodies will tend to concentrate their energies on policy areas in which its members will have the highest degree of consensus. Primarily these will be increased government funding of national, regional and local tourism research, marketing and promotion activities, the minimisation of labour costs, the minimisation of taxation on tourist businesses, and increased deregulation of the tourism industry. For example, the tourism industry is increasingly claiming that self-regulation in terms of environmental impacts is preferable to government regulation.

Having resources is not the same as mobilising them to wield successful political influence. In the tourism policy arena this is particularly the case in the conservation area, where there is widespread public support in Western countries for environmental protection measures. Business associations may use advocacy advertising in an effort to create a basis of support in the community for industry actions and positions. Where there is opposition to tourism development by local communities and/or conservation organisations, tourism businesses will often refer to the perceived economic and employment benefits of tourism. Government and voters will therefore often be faced with an apparent conflict between economic and environmental values in the decision-making process.

The effort to shape public opinion by business will usually be facilitated by a downturn in perceived loss of economic strength in a country or community. Vogel (1989) argued that business fares better politically when it can refuse social demands, and do so convincingly because of widespread fear of economic jeopardy in terms of employment and income. This may be at the macro-level, e.g. in times of general national and international economic recession, or it may be at the local level where an industry's precarious financial position, for example the casino industry in Atlantic City (see Chapter 3), may give it more power over development decisions, as employee and government stakeholders, and revenue recipients seek to keep the industry profitable (Teske and Sur 1991). Similarly, the siting of major league sports teams is also closely related to economic arguments.

Most major sports teams play in stadia that are built, maintained and improved with public funds. Local government will frequently under-price rents and provide associated infrastructure in order to support teams and to increase city status. Local hotels, restaurants and related businesses are also incorporated into the policy arena because of the benefits that they receive from visitors to stadia. In the name of the public interest, public officials will seek to retain sports franchises or gain new ones (Wong 1985). For example, in Chicago, a new stadium for the White Sox baseball team was cloaked 'in an economic development package that would not only keep the team in Chicago, but also bring an improvement in the quality of life to that neighbourhood and its residents, including those that had to be displaced for construction' (Pelissero et al. 1991: 126)

Labour organisations

The tourism industry labour force has had a history of low unionisation. This is, in major part, because of the highly seasonal, part-time and casual nature of employment in the tourism industry which is related to a high level of voluntary labour turnover and minimal on-the-job training (Shaw and Williams 1994; Hall 1995). Moves towards greater flexibility in the tourism and hospitality workplace through multi-skilling may even lead to lower levels of employee unionisation in some countries. For example, the Reo Stakis group, which has 33 hotels in the United Kingdom, ceased to recognise trades unions in the 1980s and introduced the new grade of 'multiskilled hotel employee' (Urry 1990, in Shaw and Williams 1994: 148). In Australia, similar multi-skilling arrangements have been undertaken in cooperation with the union movement. However, this was primarily because of the close political association between the trade union movement and the Labour government.

The employment trends in tourism towards a small permanent core of workers and a larger 'flexible' group of contract, casual and part-time employees means that increased rates of unionisation will be unlikely. In addition, the large number of low-skilled and unskilled positions in the tourism industry also make it easy for managers to find substitute workers should labour be withheld during a strike or industrial ban. The low levels of unionisation in the tourism industry therefore gives trade unions little leverage in negotiations with business and correspondingly little influence as an interest group in the tourism policy-making process at the macro-level.

Non-producer interest groups

Non-producer groups – public interest groups, consumer groups, conservation groups, and social justice groups – have had a dramatic impact on tourism policy-making over the last few years. The relatively high position of issues of sustainability on the contemporary tourism policy agenda is due in no small part to the activities of environmental groups, such as Greenpeace (international), World Wildlife Fund (international), the Sierra Club (United States and Canada), the National Trust (United Kingdom, Australia) and various national park and wilderness organisations. Although environmental organisations have traditionally only had an indirect involvement in tourism policy, their advocacy on conservation issues has been a part of the general policy environment within which tourism operates. For example, conservation groups seeking to establish a national park and exclude non-compatible land uses will often use tourism as part of the economic arguments for park creation (Hall 1992a).

In recent years, however, tourist groups have taken a more direct interest in tourism as the size and scale of tourism has increasingly come to impact negatively on the natural environment (McKercher 1993a, 1993b). Furthermore, the growth of ecotourism as a tourism marketing category has meant that conservation organisations have become active in monitoring, promoting or even establishing nature-based tourism operations, particularly in developing countries (Cater and Lowman 1994). Conservation and environmental interest groups are therefore playing a substantial role in tourism policy-making at both the national and international levels and are increasingly finding themselves being drawn into the institutional structure of policy-making. For example, Greenpeace was invited on to the planning team for the Sydney 2000 Olympics bid in order to assist in the promotion of the Games as a 'Green' event.

Although conservation interest groups are the major form of non-producer interest group, social justice groups are also increasingly starting to influence tourism policy. Two major types of social justice groups may be identified: native peoples' interest groups which seek either the economic benefits of tourism or to restrict tourism's impacts; or broad based social justice groups which are attempting to develop fair and responsible tourism trade. In the latter category, the British organisation Tourism Concern is slowly starting to impact on tourism policy-making, although its political strength relative to that of the wider tourism industry is minute.

Single-issue interest groups

The growth of non-producer groups at the national and international level has been matched by the growth of single-issue interest groups. The majority of single-issue interest groups operate at the local level. However, there are some notable exceptions. For example, the campaign to End Child Prostitution in Asian Tourism (ECPAT) is internationally active, and has produced notable policy successes in Australia and Germany where child sex tourism legislation has been enacted.

The majority of single-issue interest groups are established in relation to tourism development issues at the local level and are primarily resident action groups. By virtue of being single-issue groups they tend to have few resources and will usually only be able to sustain action for a short period of time. Examples of single-issue group action includes protests against resort development and protests against the bidding or hosting of mega-events such as the Olympic Games or World Fairs.

One of the characteristics of single-issue interest groups is their association with what is known as the NIMBY syndrome. NIMBY stands for 'Not In My Backyard' and refers to situations in which although there may be in principle agreement for a particular policy in a community, e.g. tourism development or the development of tourism related infrastructure such as transport links or improved sewage disposal services, the community or group of residents do not want the development in their neighbourhood. Apart from resort development, excellent examples of NIMBY include the location of airports (we want to fly but we don't want to live under the flight path) and the construction of stadia (we want to support the team but we don't want the noise and traffic problems).

NIMBY poses particularly difficult problems for government. Although tourism NIMBY are typically not of the same scale as the siting of a nuclear reactor or intractable waste dumps, they still have the capacity to cause a great deal of turbulence in the policy-making process, particularly for local government. Therefore, the ability of single-interest groups to resist unpopular siting decisions by government or the private sector will typically depend on their level of organisation, sophistication, and ability to generate wider support from other elements of the policy-making process for their cause. The next section highlights some of the key characteristics and concepts in interest group networks.

Interest group networks

The proliferation of interests in the policy process over the past two decades has not only increased the number of interest groups involved in policy-making but has also made the process more complex. Until the mid-1970s policy-making was often envisaged as occurring in sub-governments (Cigler 1991). The notion of subgovernment connotes a stable triangular alliance of policy specialists, including the 'triangle' of legislative committees, executive agencies, and interest groups, including other interests and actors. The stability of the relationship between the members of the triangle meant that the subgovernment was relatively impervious to outside influences on policy formulation and implementation. Subgovernmental dominance therefore exists where small groups of public officials and private citizens interact to make policy decisions in an issue area over extended periods of time without outside involvement or serious challenge (Ripley and Franklin 1987). In many countries and regions tourism policy-making has historically resembled the subgovernment model, given the close relationship that exists between peak industry bodies and business interests and tourism agencies. However, given the growth of non-producer and single-interest groups operating in the tourism policy field, the subgovernment model is increasingly coming under challenge.

McCool (1989) concluded that there is a continuum among sub-governments with autonomous 'iron triangles' at one end and open 'issue networks' at the other. Issue networks are structures of interaction among participants in a policy area that are marked by their transience and the absence of established centres of control (Heclo 1978). According to Heclo the term 'issue network' describes

a configuration of individuals concerned about a particular aspect of an issue and the term policy community is used more broadly to encompass the collection of issue networks within a jurisdiction. Both describe the voluntary and fluid configuration of people with varying degrees of commitment to a particular cause.

(Heclo 1978: 102)

The concept of issue networks is important for an understanding of policy formation, and agenda building in particular, because it provides insight into the critical processes which frequently determine the definition of policy issues and the articulation of policy alternatives. Alliances are formed between producer groups, non-producer interest groups, and single-interest groups and shift depending on the issues and the outcomes involved. Where network participants coalesce to advocate for particular policies, an advocacy coalition can be said to have emerged (Sabatier 1987). However, within the tourism policy-making system the creation of advocacy coalitions is becoming increasingly difficult. Coalitions require a critical mass of supporters to lead to action and the increasing complexity of the tourism policy arena works against coalition as the number of stakeholders has increased. Although coalition building in tourism is still probably easier than other policy arenas where, for example, there is a well-organised labour force, non-producer groups, such as consumer, environmental and social groups have 'discovered' tourism. The growth of tourism, with a correspondingly increased recognition of its economic, environmental and social impacts, has also led to increased political impact. As Cigler (1991) observed:

It has become more difficult to practice consensual politics due to changes in the nature of public policy, structural reforms in the policy process, and the impact of the public interest movement, which has brought a number of actors into the process who are willing to utilize 'outsider' strategies and has introduced electoral costs for legislators unwilling to pay attention to broader interests ... Many issues have been redefined ... policies are not characterized by compromise, accommodation and secrecy. Rather, they involve confrontation, a wider scope of conflict, and, often, more public scrutiny.

(Cigler 1991: 122)

The significance of interest groups in tourism policy-making

One of the great problems in examining the role of interest groups in the tourism policy-making process is deciding what the appropriate relationship between an interest group and government should be. At what point does tourism industry membership of government advisory committees or of a national, regional or local tourism agency represent a 'closing up' of the policy process to other interest groups rather than an exercise in consultation?

this co-operation between groups and bureaucrats can sometimes be a good thing. But it may sometimes be a very bad thing. These groups, used to each other's needs, may become increasingly preoccupied with each other, insensitive to the needs of outsiders, and impervious to new recruitment and to new ideas. Or the members of the various interest group elites may identify more and more with each other and less and less with the interests of the groups they represent

(Deutsch 1970: 56)

Incorporation, by which an interest group is co-opted into the formal policy-making structures of government, is a common response to interest-group demands. For example, environmental groups might be invited to sit on the boards of natural resource management agencies or recreational organisations might be invited to join the management advisory committees of national parks.

Deutsch (1970) argued that in highly pluralistic and organised societies in which incorporation is the norm, policy arenas become a cycle of alternating states of immobility (as a result of incorporation) and crisis (produced by new interest group demands from outside of the institutional structure). In order to have their demands incorporated into the policy-making process, interest groups may resort to non-conventional political tactics. For example, conservation groups throughout Western society have used direct protest actions, such as sitting in front of bulldozers and chaining themselves to trees, in order to attract media attention and therefore raise public awareness of environmental issues and their handling by government and business. Similarly, in the early 1980s, women's groups in the Philippines staged protest rallies during visits by the Japanese Prime Minister in order to draw attention to the large numbers of Japanese men travelling to the country as sex tourists. Such actions played an important role in highlighting the impacts of institutionalised prostitution in the Philippines and helped encourage legislative action on child and mail-bride prostitution (Philippine Women's Research Collective 1985; Richter 1989). Nevertheless, while direct action may be a useful technique in gaining attention for a policy issue, it is unlikely that policy shifts will result unless group demands are supported by a wider set of community values.

The relationship between interest groups and government clearly raises questions about the extent to which established policy processes lead to outcomes which are in the 'public interest' rather than simply a deal between politicians and sectional interests. There is a general consensus in Western democracies that government should avoid 'client politics' in which interests seem to have a disproportionate influence on policy areas. Mucciaroni (1991: 474) noted that 'client politics is typical of policies with diffuse costs and concentrated benefits. An identifiable group benefits from a policy, but the costs are paid by everybody or at least a large part of society'. Tourism policy is one such area, particularly in terms of the costs of tourism promotion and marketing. Typically, funding for national and regional tourism promotion comes from the public purse rather than from the industry, or is heavily subsidised in relation to the contribution from the private sector. Clearly, it is in the interests of the tourism industry to maintain this situation (refer to the case study of the Australian Tourism Industry Association and the Industries Assistance Commission Inquiry into Travel and Tourism for an example of industry influence).

Equality of access is clearly crucial in assessing how far some groups have been able to influence the policy-making process to their advantage. The next chapter deals further with some of these issues of power and the nature of public participation in planning and policy. However, it is worth noting that despite the undoubted strength of business interests in determining tourism policy, there are signs that other interests are able to influence policy settings. In particular, one would note that environmental groups have performed relatively well in pushing conservation perspectives on tourism development in recent years. Indeed, it is likely that the continued growth of non-producer group interest in tourism will further lead to reduced business influence in some areas of tourism policy-making.

Case study 3: The Australian Tourism Industry Association and the Industries Assistance Commission Inquiry into Travel and Tourism

From 1988–89 an Australian Federal Government agency, the Industries Assistance Commission (IAC) conducted an Inquiry into Travel and Tourism in Australia. The IAC invited public submissions about aspects of the tourism industry and about its national context, particularly in terms of airline and tourism industry deregulation and the appropriateness of government roles in tourism. 'Unfortunately, little of this input was evident in the Final Report' (Craik 1990: 30).

The IAC received a large number of submissions on the Australian tourism industry with particular reference to the environmental and social impacts of tourism as well as a number of industry submissions. However, in 'a classic example of clientelism' (Craik 1990), the conclusions of the final report were closely allied to the submissions of the government departments, industry associations, and the Australian Tourism Industry Association (ATIA), the peak industry body – the latter appearing to have substantial influence. The extent of the clientelism and the apparent political weight of sections of the tourism industry can be ascertained from the changes which took place between the draft report and the release of the final report.

The draft report questioned government funding of tourist promotion (a policy usually not adopted for other Australian industries) through the Australian Tourist Commission (ATC), criticised the lack of promotion effectiveness indicators, and advocated the principle of 'user pays', whereby the ATC's government funding would be reduced and it would be refor-mulated as an 'incorporated body' which could be taken over by the private tourist industry. As the IAC (1989a) stated:

Case study 3 *(continued)*

In principle, promotion should continue to the point where the gains from extra expenditure equal the cost. While the tourism sector, if left to itself, may underpromote, it is not clear that governments will get closer to the optimal level. They incur the costs, but do not reap the benefits. How are they to tell whether their promotional activities are paying off, and when new benefits cease? The incentives are reversed for the industry. Because they do not bear the costs of promotion, any benefit, however small, will be seen as a gain, whether or not there are net benefits for the economy as a whole.

(IAC 1989a: 118)

Following the release of the draft report, the tourism industry, and ATIA in particular, undertook intensive lobbying and were able to ensure that significant revisions on draft recommendations were included in the final report. The biggest about-face concerned the future of the ATC, the federally-funded tourism promotion body. As Craik (1991: 226) commented: 'The differences between the ... draft and final reports make extraordinary reading. Whereas the draft report recommended that the ATC be phased out over the next five years, the final report quoted an ATIA submission verbatim and recommended that funding be continued for five years, at which time the ATC's role should be reviewed.'

The degree to which the IAC met the needs of ATIA is also witnessed in the change of tune by Sir Frank Moore, Chairman of ATIA, towards the Inquiry. At the beginning of the Inquiry, he denounced it as a 'Treasury stooge' wanting to impose further taxes on the tourism industry. 'After the final report, he declared that the tourist industry welcomed attention from the IAC because it was "neutral" and had "no pre-conceived ideas". The IAC was, he said, "dispassionate", "divorced from self-interest", and had a "balanced view of industry" ' (Craik 1990: 31).

The conflict between interest groups in tourism policy formulation was most clearly seen in concerns over social and environmental issues. Despite being charged with assessing the various economic, cultural, social and environmental impacts of

Case study 3 *(continued)*

tourism, social issues only received two pages of discussion in the final report, while the issue of the environment was assigned the penultimate chapter (IAC 1989b). Furthermore, the IAC examined social and environmental issues purely in economic terms. Longer-term social and environmental concerns and issues of sustainability were, therefore, all but ignored in the final report. According to Craik (1990: 42), 'ATIA now regards the IAC Report as "the bible of the industry".' Others see it as 'a blueprint that endorses narrow self-interests at the expense of public interests'. Either way it is apparent that the IAC report represented a relatively closed policy-making process in terms of representing the various interests that exist in tourism policy. 'In short, the IAC Report looked like an unlikely alliance between industry advocates and neo-classical economists, each attempting to push barrows that, although adopting different courses, coincided in strategies to boost the development of the tourism industry' (Craik 1990: 30).

Summary

This chapter has indicated the nature of interest groups and their prospective influence on tourism policy. It has highlighted the strength of business interests in determining tourism policy settings and the weakness of organised labour. It was also noted that non-producer interest groups such as conservation, consumer, rate-payer, and public interest organisations and single-interest groups were increasingly influencing tourism policy and were likely to continue to do so in the future. In theoretical terms it was noted that this was reflected in a change in political structure from a subgovernment 'triangle' to what was termed an 'issue network'. However, to what extent this reflects a lessening of the 'incorporation' of industry interests in tourism policy or 'client politics' remains somewhat problematic.

Of major significance in terms of the policy process is the growing number of interest groups operating in the tourism policy environment and the corresponding complexity of policy-making. The complexity and number of stakeholders clearly provides a major challenge to government as well, of course, as to the interest groups themselves in the achievement of their objectives and the possibility of consensual politics.

Questions for review and discussion

1 How has the increased number and range of tourism-related interest groups affected the policy-making process?
2 What are the differences between an interest group and a political party?
3 Is tourism policy-making best described as a subgovernment or an issue network?
4 To what extent is tourism policy determined by business interests rather than the public interest?

Guide to further reading

On general interest group literature see Cigler and Loomis (1986), which contains a number of review chapters and case studies of interest group activity; Schlozman and Tierney (1986); and Salisbury *et al.* (1987). A more detailed discussion of the concepts of subgovernment and issue networks is to be found in Berry (1989).

Useful case studies of tourism-related interest group activity are to be found in Craik (1990) and Pelissero *et al.* (1991). Although a little dated, the articles by Hayes (1981) and Airey (1984) provide some interesting details on business influence on United States tourism policy.

5
Who wins and who loses?
Aspects of power in tourism policy-making

Policy is deliberate coercion – statements attempting to set forth the purpose, the means, the subjects, and the objects of coercion ... Inevitably there is an element of coercion in collective life. Organization is a means of stabilizing relations among members of a collectivity so that, despite efforts of some to displace costs on the collective, a rough sharing of the costs of collective benefits can be made. Administration is a means of routinizing coercion. Government is a means of legitimizing it. Power is simply the relative share a person or group appears to have in shaping and directing the instruments of coercion.

(Lowi 1970: 314–315)

Power and tourism policy

As was apparent when we examined the various dimensions of interest group behaviour, there are winners and loses in public policy. A prescriptive–rationalist approach to public policy would see the decisions of government as being part of an inherently rational policy-making process in which goals, values and objectives can be ranked and identified after the collection and systematic evaluation of the necessary data (Wilson 1941). However, this approach to policy analysis, though influential, is extremely misleading as it fails to recognise the inherently political nature of public policy. As Fischer and Forester (1993) recognised,

> policy and planning arguments are intimately involved with relations of power and the exercise of power, including the concerns of some and excluding others, distributing responsibility as well as causality, imputing blame as well as efficacy, and employing particular political strategies and problem framing and not others.
>
> (Fischer and Forester 1993: 7)

Politics and public policy are inextricably linked (see Chapter 1). Politics is about power, who gets what, where, how and why (Lasswell 1936). Decisions affecting tourism policy, the nature of government involvement in tourism, the structure of tourism agencies, the nature of tourism development, and community involvement in tourism planning and policy all emerge from a political process. As noted in Chapter 1, this process involves the values of actors (individuals, interest groups and public and private organisations) in a struggle for power relative to the public policy process. So far we have discussed the institutional arrangements, values, and interest groups involved in policy-making. This chapter examines the exercise of power that determines the values and interests that 'win' in the policy arena.

The concept of power

Ideas of power have been little explored in tourism studies (Britton 1991), yet the concept of power is a central concept in the social sciences. 'Power' is an 'essentially contested' concept – a concept whose application is inherently a matter of dispute (Gallie 1955–56; Molnar and Rogers 1982). Power may be conceptualised as 'all forms of successful control by A over B – that is, of A securing B's compliance' (Lukes 1974: 17). The use of the concept of power is inextricably linked to a given set of value assumptions which predetermine the range of its application. Lukes constructed a typology of power and related concepts in an effort to clarify their meaning and relationship (Table 5.1). Lukes identified three different approaches, or dimensions, in the analysis of power, each focusing on different aspects of the decision-making process: a one-dimensional view emphasising observable, overt behaviour, conflict, and decision-making (Dahl 1958, 1961, 1967, 1983); a two-dimensional view which recognises decisions and non-decisions, observable (overt or covert) conflict, and which represents a qualified critique of the behavioural stance of the one-dimensional view (Bachrach and Baratz 1962, 1963, 1970; Bachrach 1969–70; Wolfinger

1971; Morriss 1972); and a three-dimensional view which focuses on decision-making and control over the political agenda (not necessarily through decisions), and which recognises observable (overt or covert) and latent conflict (Crenson 1971; Lukes 1974).

Table 5.1 Typology of power and related concepts

Concept	Meaning
Authority	B complies because he recognises that A's command is reasonable in term of his own values, either because its content is legitimate and reasonable or because it has been arrived at through a legitimate and reasonable procedure
Coercion	Exists where A secures B's compliance by the threat of deprivation where there is a conflict over values or course of action between A and B
Force	A achieves his objectives in the face of B's non-compliance
Influence	Exists where A, without resorting to either a tacit or overt threat of severe deprivation, causes B to change his course of action
Manipulation	Is an 'aspect' or sub-concept of force (and distant from coercion, power, influence and authority) since here compliance is forthcoming in the absence of recognition on the compiler's part either of the source or the exact nature of demand upon him
Power	All forms of successful control by A over B – that is, of A securing B's compliance

Source: Bachrach and Baratz (1970: 24, 28, 30, 34); Lukes (1974: 17)

Each of the three dimensions arises out of, and operates within, a particular political perspective as the concept of power is 'ineradicably value-dependent' (Lukes 1974: 26). For example, a one-dimensional, pluralist conception of the tourism policy-making process, such as that which underlies the notion of community-based tourism planning (Murphy 1985, 1988; Haywood 1988), will focus on different aspects of the decision-making process than structuralist conceptions of politics which highlight social relations within the consumption of tourist services (Urry 1990; Hall 1994a). As Britton recognised

> we need a theorisation that explicitly recognises, and unveils, tourism as a predominantly capitalistically organised activity driven by the inherent and defining social dynamics of that system, with its attendant production, social, and ideological relations. An analysis of

how the tourism production system markets and packages people is a lesson in the political economy of the social construction of 'reality' and social construction of place, whether from the point of view of visitors and host communities, tourism capital (and the 'culture industry'), or the state – with its diverse involvement in the system.
(Britton 1991: 475)

Given the need to understand the dominant groups and ideologies operating within the tourism political system (also referred to as the black box of decision-making (Easton 1965)), the use of a wide conception of power, capable of identifying decisions, non-decisions and community political structure, will provide the most benefit in the analysis of the political dimensions of tourism (Hall 1994a).

Setting the tourism policy agenda

Political issues have an organisational aspect. As Crozier (1964: 107) noted, 'The behaviour and attitudes of people and groups within an organisation cannot be explained without reference to the power relationships existing among them.' Therefore, research on tourism policy needs to connect the substance of policy to the process of policy-making including the relationship between power, structure and values. Studies of tourism policy-making should therefore attempt to understand not only the politically imposed limitations upon the scope of policy- and decision-making, but also the political framework within which the research process itself takes place.

One of the issues which arises in the identification of the different dimensions of power is the manner in which the policy agenda may be set or framed prior to various interests being involved in policy debates. As Schattschneider (1960: 66) argued, 'The definition of alternatives is the supreme instrument of power.' Problem definition is

the processes by which an issue . . . having been recognised as such and placed on the public policy agenda, is perceived by various interested parties; further explored, articulated . . . and in some cases, given an authoritative or at least provisionally accepted definition in terms of its likely causes, components, and consequences.
(Hogwood and Gunn 1984: 109)

Problems and, hence, policy alternatives can be defined before they reach the policy arena in two primary ways. First, is by way of a dominant ideology or set of values which defines the parameters within which problems are defined and discussed, and solutions conceived and carried out. This ideology may be a state or an organisational ideology. For example, in the case study of the Industries Assistance Commission Inquiry into Travel and Tourism discussed in Chapter 4, the Commission had a very strong economic orientation and an organisational culture which emphasised the role of the marketplace. Therefore, the organisational values of the Commission and its members provided the dominant values to be found in the analysis and research conducted under the terms of reference for the Inquiry (Craik 1990).

The second means is through the setting of the rules by which policy debate is carried out, in other words, the 'rules of the game'. The 'rules of the game' are 'a set of predominant values, beliefs, rituals and institutional procedures that operate systematically and consistently to the benefit of certain persons and groups at the expense of others'. Those who benefit 'are placed in a preferred position to defend and promote their vested interests' (Bachrach and Baratz 1970: 43–44). The rules of the game affect the behaviour of groups:

> As intervening factors between the individual political actor and the generalized norms of the political system, these rules have certain distinctive attributes and comprise an important part of the policy-maker's environment. . . . [These rules are linked to] the values, myths and beliefs that tie a people together in a community and the overall pattern of power and authority relationships in the society as a whole.
>
> (Anderson 1976: 278)

Therefore, instutionalised rules condition the cognitive and normative understandings of different actors thereby facilitating some strategies while constraining others. Institutionalised rules refer to accepted ways of viewing how society works and consequent prescriptions for attaining objectives. For example, a parliamentary or congressional committee may be established to enquire into certain issues surrounding the tourism industry, but the terms of reference which are set by the committee will determine the scope of their policy discussions. As Schattschneider (1960: 71) has written: 'All forms of political organisation have a bias in favour of the exploitation of some kinds of conflict, and the suppression of others, because organisation is the mobilisation of bias. Some issues are organised into politics while some others are organised out.'

The challenge for groups whose interests are not met in the definition of policy alternatives is to try and change the policy agenda. Nelson

(1984: 20) distinguished between three types of political agendas which are drawn up to consider matters of public policy. The first is the governmental agenda which consists of what issues government institutions are considering. The second is the popular agenda which is made up of the general public's awareness. The third is the professional agenda which is the awareness of an informed public which promotes a particular view of a specific issue. According to Michaels (1992: 242), a policy community in the form of various interest groups 'operates with a professional agenda but seeks to have their issue placed on the governmental or public agenda either directly or by using a popular agenda as a means to get the attention of governmental decision-makers'. However, such a statement assumes that the policy agenda is relatively open, and that entry to the policy-making process is available to all interests. In some policy issues, particularly those relating to non-economic factors or those areas on which there is widespread public support, then this may be possible. Nevertheless, when policy issues are primarily economic in orientation, the agenda will be more closed because of the dominance of economic thinking in policy settings. As the next section highlights, many apparently 'open' areas of policy-making have many restrictions placed on them.

Power in tourism policy-making

Pluralism refers to the belief that power is relatively dispersed in a society and that policy-making institutions are open to influence by a wide range of interest groups. As a result, political decisions are reached through a process of bargaining, negotiation and compromise between the various interests involved. Power is therefore diffused through a society. Different centres of power exist, constant negotiations among different centres of power are necessary to make decisions, minorities can veto decisions through use of their voting power, and memberships of interest groups overlap. According to Dahl (1967: 24), 'The fundamental axiom in the theory and practice of American pluralism is, I believe, this: Instead of a single center of sovereign power there must be multiple centers of power, none of which is or can be wholly sovereign.'

The pluralist account of power, of which Robert Dahl provided the clearest exposition, has been strongly criticised on several counts (Lukes 1974; DeAngelis and Parkin 1980). First, while Dahl (1967: 38) argued that 'few groups in the United States who are determined to influence the government – certainly few in any groups who are organised, active and persistent – lack the capacity and opportunity to influence some officials somewhere in the political system in order to obtain some of their goals', it is clearly possible to identify a number of interests that are relatively unorganised and therefore do not carry much power as an interest group, e.g. the poor, ethnic minorities, indigenous peoples and the unemployed. Second, as noted in the previous chapter, some interest groups, particularly business, are demonstrably more powerful in the policy-making environment. Third, voting power has only limited capacity as a means of protest as election issues and electoral choice are usually quite narrow. Fourth, while there are undoubtedly a number of interest groups operating in the policy system, power is unevenly divided between them. Fifth, there will be a bias by government towards interest groups that are recognised by government and consulted by them, e.g. peak industry bodies and other producer groups. Single-interest groups normally find it harder to obtain government recognition. Sixth, any consensus in favour of a policy or values will be favouring certain interests over others. This final criticism is closely related to Crenson's (1971: 178) argument that there are 'politically imposed limitations upon the scope of decision-making', such that 'decision-making activities are channelled and directed by the process of non-decision-making'. Pluralism is 'no guarantee of political openness or popular sovereignty', and 'neither the study of [overt] decision-making' nor the existence of 'visible diversity' will tell us anything about 'those groups and issues which may have been shut out of a town's political life' (Crenson 1971: 181).

Power, place and urban tourism

Place, and representations of place, is a social process. Urban heritage tourism is explicitly related to notions of place. 'There is no better stage set for the spectacle of capital than a recycled mercantile area' (Boyer 1992: 201). Urban heritage conservation, particularly waterfront redevelopment schemes such as those in London, Liverpool, New York and Baltimore, is interconnected to the power relationships that exist within and outside of a community. However, within such relationships, it is apparent that the heritage of the losers is often lost or, at least, under-represented. The past becomes a sanitised pastiche of its former self as the sights, sounds, and smells of the old waterfront are banished, and retailers have a diminished relationship with a maritime past. The preservation of historic waterfronts and the creation of festival marketplaces occurs merely as props for larger enterprises within the context of contemporary patterns of consumption. As Boyer (1992: 203) noted with respect to New York's South Street Seaport which had set out to evoke the Fulton Fish Market, 'Only the removal of the fish from the fish market finally made the "historic" tableau commercially viable.'

Heritage, as with place, is a social construct. However, the vast majority of heritage tourism research has failed to identify the political dimensions of the social process(es) by which heritage and place are constructed. Heritage is a major component of place promotion. Nevertheless, it is somewhat ironic that the very places which have sought to differentiate themselves have ended up looking the same, what may be described as serial monotony or the serial replication of homogeneity (Boyer 1988; Harvey 1993).

As Harvey (1993: 8) asked, 'The question immediately arises as to why people accede to the construction of their places by such a process.' In many cases they of course do not, because communities may resist development. For example, 'political battles between residents and specially created redevelopment authorities have punctuated the urban renewal of Australian waterfronts' (Kelly and McConville 1991: 91). However, while short-term opposition did save the physical fabric of many Australian inner-city communities, it is worth while noting that the social fabric has been changed through gentrification and touristification of many areas leaving only heritage façades. Indeed, Harvey (1993) also notes that resistance has not checked the overall process of place competition. A mixture of coercion and co-option centred around maintenance of real estate values, assumptions regarding employment and investment generation, and an assumption that growth is automatically good, has led to the creation of local growth coalitions (see Chapter 3).

> Coercion arises either through interplace competition for capital investment and employment (accede to the capitalist's demands or go out of business; create a 'good business climate' or lose jobs) or more simply, through the direct political repression and oppression of dissident voices (from cutting off media access to the more violent tactics of the construction mafias in many of the world's cities).
>
> (Harvey 1993: 9)

The central concerns of politics and power are sometimes apparent in heritage tourism; more often they are not. Ideology, values and power relations are inscribed not only in space through the process of uneven development (Harvey 1993: 9; Lefebvre 1991), but also through the representation of place. As Norkunas (1993) described with respect to heritage tourism in Monterey (see Case study 4):

The ruling class carefully controls the form and content of historical re-creations and tourist landscapes, legitimizing itself by projecting its own contemporary sociocultural values upon the past. This struggle, the tension between groups with power and groups with varying but lesser degrees of power, is replayed in the many spheres in which the public enactment of identity is staged. The erection or non-erection of statuary is a physical manifestation of that tension; nostalgic reinterpretations of socially condemnatory fiction, which results in a humorous caricature of poverty is yet another manifestation of this struggle. Dominance is expressed not in terms of physical coercion but as rhetoric.

(Norkunas 1993: 97)

The creation and representation of tourism places therefore needs to be understood in a far wider context than has generally hitherto been the case. The application of models of community participation in tourism planning, which assume the pluralistic allocation of power within a community, may unwittingly serve to reinforce existing power structures and representations of history to the exclusion of other interests. In the case of many ethnic and working-class communities who face the extinction of their past, 'their systematic exclusion from official history fragments the community so that feelings of alienation and "loss of soul" are experienced most deeply by minorities' (Norkunas 1993: 99).

Research into tourism therefore needs to consider the means by which power structures have potentially served to lead to a one-dimensional representation of heritage and place to visitors, which ignores the complex range of place histories that often exist. By revealing the richness of place and the power structures that often serve to restrict historical representation to visitors, students of tourism may well reinforce the uniqueness that comes from place complexity rather than allow places to submit to the serial monotony of contemporary place competition.

Case study 4: Power, place and the heritage of Monterey

Tourism redefines social and political realities. Advertising and visitation create images of place which also create expectancies on the part of the visitor, and which, in turn, may reinforce representations of place. Destinations may therefore become caught in a tourist gaze from which they cannot readily escape unless they are willing to abandon their status as a destination. 'Policies which are used to attract tourists, lengthen their stay, and increase their expenditures also function to redefine social realities. As definitions are imposed from without, the socio-cultural reality which arises out of everyday life becomes further consumed' (Papson 1981: 233). Tourism development, marketing, routing and zoning affects notions of place. The organisation of history in tourist settings transforms the cultural and historical life of communities and, hence, transforms place itself.

Monterey, California, provides a valuable example of the political nature of heritage. Monterey has a substantial heritage tourism industry that is based on the historic significance of the region in terms of United States expansionism, and a literary and industrial heritage in the form of Cannery Row, made famous by Steinbeck, and Fisherman's Wharf.

Different tourist landscapes, such as those in Monterey, whether they are historic or commercial, can be read as distinct cultural texts, a kind of outdoor museum which displays the artefacts of a community and society. Each of these tourist cultural texts reveal certain value assumptions and power relationships which underlie the tourist environment as a form of cultural production. Indeed, Norkunas (1993: 10) notes that the 'ideology of the powerful is systematically embedded in the institutions and public texts of tourism and history'.

The rich and complex ethnic history of Monterey is almost completely absent in the 'official' historic tours and the residences available for public viewing. In Monterey, as in many other parts of the world, heritage is presented in the form of the houses of the aristocracy or elite. Historically significant houses are also highlighted from this perspective. History is 'flattened' and conflicting histories are suppressed, thereby creating a simplified

Case study 4 *(continued)*

generalised image which is consumed by the visitor. 'This synopsis of the past into a digestible touristic presentation eliminates any discussion of conflict; it concentrates instead on a sense of resolution. Opposed events and ideologies are collapsed into statements about the forward movement and rightness of history' (Norkunas 1993: 36). However, this occurs with little or no overt conflict over heritage representation. Heritage is not contested in the public sphere. Despite there being 'democratic' institutions and channels for the representation of diversity, conflicts and issues are ignored in the public history of Monterey. Therefore, what and who gets reproduced 'is the image of elite Americans of European descent who control, and have always controlled the destiny of the city . . . public history texts as well as tourist texts are involved in a form of dominance, a hegemonic discourse about the past that legitimates the ideology and power of present groups' (Norkunas 1993: 26).

The recent industrial past has also been de-emphasised in the heritage product of Monterey. As in many Western urban centres, economic restructuring within the new global economy has led to the demise of many industrial operations, such as canning. The industrial waterfront has now become a leisure space combining shopping and entertainment with residential and tourist development. Industrial heritage is typically an essential component of waterfront redevelopment. Heritage precincts are established which tell the reader the economic significance of the area, not of the lives of those who contributed to wealth generation and place development. Narratives of labour, class, and ethnicity are typically replaced by romance and nostalgia. Overt conflict, whether between ethnic groups, classes or, more particularly, in terms of industrial and labour disputes, is either ignored or glossed over in 'official' tourist histories. The overt conflict of the past has been reinterpreted by local elites to create a new history in which heritage takes a linear, conflict-free form. In the case of Monterey, the past is reinterpreted through the physical transformation of the canneries. 'Reinterpreting the past has allowed the city to effectively erase from the record the industrial era and

Case study 4 *(continued)*

---

the working class culture it engendered. Commentary on the industrial era remains only in the form of touristic interpretations of the literature of John Steinbeck' (Norkunas 1993: 50–51).

The Monterey experience is repeated time and time again throughout the Western World. From Victoria and Vancouver in British Columbia to Liverpool and the London Docklands in the United Kingdom, and from Hobart and Sydney in Australia to Auckland and Wellington in New Zealand, the urban heritage waterfront has been developed as a means of rejuvenating inner-city areas and of solving urban problems such as the environment and overcrowding. However, the political dimensions of heritage representation and the simplification of place have been little considered. As Boyer (1992) observed

> in both the tourist industry and historic preservation, there seems to be an attempt (not wholly successful) to unify and heighten the sense of the present by emphasizing the break with the past and with tradition, or to justify a particular aspect of the present by emphasizing a related aspect of the past. In the reconstructed seaport, do we concentrate on the ingenuity of the mechanics or the exoticness of the imports, on the wealth of the merchants or the poverty that led seamen to indenture themselves? Everything is significant. Museums, historic zones, and city tableaux present highly particular stagings of the past.
>
> (Boyer 1992: 199)

Public participation issues in tourism planning and policy

Public participation is widely regarded as an essential ingredient in tourism planning and policy-making (Murphy 1985; Inskeep 1991; Gunn 1994). Public participation refers to 'decision making by the target group, the general public, relevant interest groups, or other types of decision making by the target group, the general public, relevant interest groups, or other types of decision makers whose involvement appeals to our desire to use democratic procedures for achieving given goals' (Nagel 1990: 1056). However, to which public are we referring?

Awareness of the political dimensions of tourism, and more particularly the uneven allocation of power in a society or a community,
should caution us about the representativeness of outcomes of tourism
planning exercises. As this and the previous chapter have indicated,
certain interests are often better able to achieve their objectives than
others not only because of their greater resources, but also because of
their ability to influence the direction of tourism policy. In tourism
planning and policy-making it is inequality rather than equality that is
the order of the day.

Inequality of access to those in control of resources, and hence
inequality of opportunity to exert pressure, is neither accidental nor
the result of a deliberate conspiracy of the wicked or the selfish; it
is unavoidable in a complex society with an elaborate division of
labour operating in a world of which a general attribute is scarcity
(of time, effort and ability, as well as of goods); the degree and
importance of the inequality will vary, but not the fact of it.
(Moodie and Studdert-Kennedy 1970: 71)

Public participation in tourism planning may be more a form of
placation than a means of giving power to communities to form their
own decisions (Haywood 1988). In addition, participation ought not to
be assumed to affect planning outcomes. Alternatives may have already
been defined before public participation began, while any changes
which do occur may simply be changes at the margin. Therefore, notions
of representation and responsiveness in tourism planning and policy-
making need to be assessed in the light of the reality or unreality of
participation (deLeon 1994).

According to Fischer (1990), genuine political participation requires

a political system . . . in which each citizen is able to authentically
engage in the political processes of policy decision making. Speech
and argumentation are the basic media of these processes; each
citizen must, therefore, have significant voice in them. The outcome
of the deliberative process, a democratic decision, must be founded
on the most persuasive argument.
(Fischer 1990: 347)

The importance of the content and context of policy argument has
been highlighted in several recent works (Majone 1989; Fischer and
Forester 1993; Forester 1993; Hall 1994a). However, this approach is still
in the minority in tourism planning and policy analysis, the dominant

approach to which ignores values. Nevertheless, as Majone (1989: 6) argued, 'the essential need today is an improvement in the methods and conditions of critical debate and their institutionalisation at all levels of policy-making'.

Fishkin's (1991) three dimensions of democracy: deliberation, nontyranny, and political equality, provide a basis for assessing the adequacy of exercises in public participation. However, in order for such dimensions to be achieved, tourism policy analysts and planners will need both to be proactive in their design of planning systems and understand the political structure they are operating in. Urban planners have described such systems as 'participatory design' or 'advocacy planning' (Forester 1988). In the case of urban planning, 'advocacy planning means speaking for those who will actually use the building, instead of doing research about them for those who hold the power. It means helping people in a community do their own planning' (Goleman 1992, in deLeon 1994: 205). Such an approach will challenge many ideas about the role of government in the tourism planning and policy process, particularly with respect to the roles of the bureaucratic 'expert' and interest groups. Nevertheless, 'at worst', it 'will support others who fear that the rational actor, the economic man, is an untrustworthy companion, and urge the search for better mileposts' (deLeon 1994: 209).

Summary

This chapter has emphasised the critical role that power plays in tourism policy. The concept of power was reviewed and three concepts of power were identified: a one-dimensional view emphasising observable, overt behaviour, conflict, and decision-making (a pluralist perspective); a two-dimensional view which recognises decisions and non-decisions, and which represents a qualified critique of the behavioural stance of the one-dimensional view; and a three-dimensional view which focuses on decision-making and control over the political agenda (not necessarily through decisions), and which recognises observable and latent conflict. These three faces of power were used to highlight the manner in which the tourism policy agenda may be set. Finally, the role of power relationships in tourism policy-making were discussed with specific reference to urban tourism, a case study of tourism in Monterey and public participation issues in tourism planning and policy.

Power is clearly a key element in understanding how decisions are made and why certain values are excluded from tourism policy. The challenge for many involved in tourism studies is to acknowledge the centrality of power in tourism policy, and its relationship to values, interests and institutional arrangements. In the absence of such acknowledgement, much tourism research will continue to be blind to the critical role of argument in the policy process and maintain its supposedly value-neutral appraisal of tourism policy.

Questions for review and discussion

1 What are the major characteristics of the three dimensions of power identified by Lukes (1974)?
2 Is it possible for public participation to represent the public interest?
3 Should tourism planners or tourism policy analysts assume the role of advocates in the tourism policy-making process?

Guide to further reading

Lukes (1974) provides an excellent introduction to the concept of power. Students wanting a more detailed discussion of the various dimensions of power should consult Dahl (1958, 1961, 1967) on pluralist approaches; Bachrach and Baratz (1962, 1963, 1970), Wolfinger (1971), and Morriss (1972) on decisions and non-decisions, and critiques of the one-dimensional view; and Crenson (1971) and Lukes (1974) on the three-dimensional view. The third dimension of power bears significant parallels with the work of Michel Foucault on power which has received considerable exposure in recent years, particularly with respect to the concept of post-modernism. However, the agency exerting power is located locally in the work of Lukes and globally in the writings of Foucault. See Foucault (1972) for a further discussion of his notion of power. On the roles of power relationships in tourism see Britton (1991), Norkunas (1993), Harvey (1993) and Hall (1994a). The work of Norkunas provides an excellent detailed example of the operation of the second and third dimensions of power in tourism settings.

6
Monitoring and evaluating tourism public policy

As Wildavsky so cogently argues, evaluation is inherently political, and the acceptance of evaluation requires a 'community of men who share values' . . . the requirements that must be met and the sacrifices made for an organisation to indulge in evaluative activity are so severe that they are rarely met.

(Jenkins 1978: 228)

Introduction

The systematic evaluation of tourism public policy is a sadly neglected aspect of tourism planning, management and development. Given the dynamic nature of tourism in developed and undeveloped societies, it has become increasingly critical for tourism policies to be monitored and evaluated. If the circumstances under which plans and policies are implemented are constantly changing in response to internal and external political and social forces (see Figures 1.1 and 1.2), it seems logical that policies should evolve (during their formulation and imple-mentation) in a way which takes such changes into account. However, as evaluation is often neglected, it is not surprising that many writers (e.g. Murphy 1985; Hall and McArthur 1993; Jenkins 1993a, 1993b; Gunn 1994) lament that tourism policies:

- are *ad hoc* or incremental;
- lack appropriate goals, and specific and well-targeted objectives;

- are based on dubious assumptions that tourism will promote regional development and help in restructuring local economies;
- give insufficient attention to local resident involvement in the tourism policy-making process; and
- ignore the natural environments which are threatened by much tourism development despite legislative and administrative arrangements overtly supporting conservation measures. In particular, major projects are highly politicised and conveniently fast-tracked when the economic and/or political need is great, and when the political power is willing.

Challenges to government activity generally, and tourism specifically, arise from questions about the overall effectiveness of government action. Popular concern about tourism policies is slowly being reinforced by a growing scholarly literature which has expressed doubt about the success of government policies and programmes in terms of realising promised outcomes. This chapter, therefore, is both descriptive and prescriptive in tone. It advocates the adoption of monitoring and evaluation objectives and techniques for all tourism policies. In doing so, it examines key definitions and concepts, outlines the importance of monitoring and evaluation, presents a model for tourism policy evaluation and discusses some of the problems confronted in evaluating tourism policy. This chapter does not provide a discussion of evaluation techniques such as cost–benefit analysis or cost-accounting. Readers are referred to the Guide to Further Reading for references concerning those techniques.

Monitoring and evaluation: key concepts and definitions

The literature on 'evaluation' is extensive, but there is no widely accepted definition of 'evaluation'. Thus, evaluative studies vary greatly in their comprehensiveness, methodologies and analysis of data. Dye (1992), for example, provides an interesting and detailed discussion of policy evaluation, but his work is somewhat limited. According to Dye (1992: 354), 'Policy evaluation is learning about *the consequences of public policy*'. He goes to some lengths to outline the difference between policy and programme evaluation, with the latter referred to as 'a comprehensive evaluation of the entire system under consideration' (1992: 354). Dye's definition and advocacy of policy evaluation as a procedure concerned with impacts or consequences is simplistic and ignores the political system (see Jenkins's (1978) model).

'The word 'evaluation' needs careful definition. To most lay observers, it conveys a connotation of economic criteria . . . But essentially, evaluation consists of *any process which seeks to order preferences.*' (Hall 1982: 288). Hall's definition of evaluation is insightful for two principal reasons. First, many other definitions of evaluation confine evaluation to the 'what happened after the policy was implemented' phase (e.g. Dye 1992). There is no reason as to why evaluation cannot be undertaken before a policy is put into effect or implemented. For example, it would seem to make good sense to include an objective whereby responses to policy *proposals* are evaluated. 'Because errors are to be expected projects should be planned to facilitate early detection and correction' (Hollick 1993: 125). The time to consider evaluation is at the options selection and programme design stages (Hall and McArthur 1993). Second, Hall's (1982) definition acknowledges that 'evaluation is not simply concerned with carrying out technically correct evaluations; it has to be concerned with how evaluation results are consumed and utilized' (Hogwood and Gunn 1984: 220). Tourism policy evaluation should therefore be concerned with who requested the evaluation, why the evaluation was requested, the estimation, assessment or appraisal of policy, including its development, content, implementation and effects, and the manner in which that evaluation will be consumed and utilised. Evaluations of policy must consider *why* who got what and where, and the outcomes and impacts of policy. That said, goals and objectives may be ambiguous or covert and therefore difficult to detect. This in itself means policy evaluation must go beyond simply measuring outcomes and impacts with respect to goals and objectives.

In this chapter, tourism policy evaluation is an activity which is designed to collect, analyse and interpret information concerning the need for policy and the formulation, implementation, outcomes and impact of policies. Evaluations are undertaken for administrative, managerial and political purposes, for planning and policy development, and to meet fiscal accountability (Rossi *et al.* 1979). The roles of policy monitoring and evaluation are presented in Table 6.1.

From the above discussion, it should be clear that meaningful tourism policy evaluation requires: (1) an initial specification of what policy delivery is to encompass; (2) that decisions and actions throughout the policy process be specified and recorded; and (3) that outputs, impacts and recipient responses be identified and duly noted. The constant monitoring of the tourism policy process alerts decision-makers and policy-makers to situations in which public officials carry out different

Table 6.1 The roles of monitoring and evaluation in the tourism policy-making process

1 Assessing the degree of need for government intervention and policy.
2 Continuous function of the policy-making process to enlighten, clarify and improve policy.
3 Conceptual and operational assistance to decision-makers and policy-makers, particularly as shifts in implementation and target needs and expectations occur.
4 Specification of policy outcomes and impacts.
5 Assessing or measuring the efficiency and cost-effectiveness of tourism policies in terms of the financial, human and capital resources.
6 Accountability reporting for resource allocation, distribution and redistribution.
7 Symbolic reasons (to demonstrate that something is being done).
8 Political reasons.

Source: Adapted from Haynes (1974), Rossi *et al.* (1979), Graycar (1983) and Owen (1993)
Note: Each of these roles may be closely linked in any given situation

activities from those envisaged, or perhaps when policies fails to reach intended clients. In other words, simply to 'evaluate the programme in terms of its original objectives might lead to a conclusion that the policy was a failure, yet this might be misleading since the policy as originally envisaged might not actually have been put into effect' (Hogwood and Gunn 1984: 220). Policy failure or success could be the result of various aspects of policy design (e.g. ambiguous statements of objectives and intent), policy implementation (e.g. bureaucratic discretion or uncontrollable global forces), or from unforeseen forces (e.g. economic, political and social) creating changes in public need. Such suggestions should alert students of tourism to the importance of studying tourism policies at a number of levels, as well as pinpoint the need for comprehensive monitoring and evaluation of tourism policies.

The concept of policy evaluation can present problems in terms of deciding what to evaluate and when to evaluate within often considerable resource constraints. Many policies are extensive and, as discussed later in this chapter, their effects may be difficult to detect. Rossi *et al.* (1979) discuss four main features or categories of evaluation which can be applied to the evaluation of tourism policies (also see Pal 1992: 43). First, government intervention is a response to a problem to which research effort is directed in terms of assessing and specifying the degree of need for policy and action. Second, there are questions pertaining to monitoring as information is required on the policy process, particularly as to policy progress and implementation. Third, at some stage attention must be given to specifying policy outcomes and impacts. Finally, questions may be raised regarding the efficiency of tourism policy and its opportunity costs. Each of the above aspects are critical to the future development of tourism public policy, for government accountability, and for any assessment of the benefits and costs associated with tourism public policy. Furthermore, each stage highlights the importance of constantly monitoring the policy process, and of seeing evaluation as more than specifying tourism policy outcomes or the measurement or assessment of impact.

Comprehensive policy evaluation of tourism policies is rare probably because (1) competition over limited government funds is often fierce and, hence, few resources are given to evaluations of public policies, and (2) bureaucrats tend to focus more on day-to-day decisions than on strategic planning. Therefore, in considering policy evaluation

two distinctions should be kept in mind. The first is between *comprehensive* and *non-comprehensive* evaluation. The former would include each one of the four major categories of evaluation [discussed above] in assessing a programme or policy. Most evaluation research is of the second variety, for reasons of expense. The second distinction is between *summative* and *formative evaluations*. Summative [policy] evaluation is a final assessment to aid decisions about continuing, discontinuing, adopting, or rejecting [policies]. It does not show ways of improving [policy] performance. Formative evaluations are designed to do precisely this: to isolate different [policy] components and assess their contribution to overall [policy] impact.

(Pal 1992: 43)

By way of example, Table 6.2 lists some of the general techniques for the evaluation and control of special events which were endorsed by the Canadian Government Office of Tourism. Techniques 1 to 7 in Table 6.2 can be categorised as formative evaluations which contribute to the overall policy process and a final (or summative) assessment (Technique 8) of the event. The next section discusses the importance of the monitoring and evaluation of tourism policies.

The importance of monitoring and evaluation in tourism policy

Much attention has been directed to policy implementation – what happens after policies are formulated (legislation passed or directives issued) – since the early 1970s. Pressman and Wildavsky's (1973) publication entitled *Implementation* is a classic text which sparked

Table 6.2 General techniques for the evaluation and control of events

Technique
1   Each committee records all the major problems encountered, the solutions reached, and a subsequent evaluation of the solution.
2   Copies of all forms and form letters such as fund-raising letters and registration forms should be filed.
3   Copies of all publicity pieces produced such as tickets, booklets and fliers should be filed.
4   The mailing list should be filed.
5   Audited financial statements with a comparison to budgets should be reported and the reasons for being over or under the budget stated.
6   Attendance figures need to be reported including where the audience came from, what they liked, and how they heard about the event.
7   Figures on local commercial activity during the event such as traffic counts, petrol station sales, hotel/motel occupancy rates, restaurant sales, and general merchants' sales, are most useful for giving the festival economic credibility in a particular locale.
8   An overall evaluation of the event by the executive committee in terms of its financial success, acceptability of individual events, and the success of individual publicity and promotion strategies is invaluable for the planning and management of any future event.

Source: After Canadian Government Office of Tourism (1982: 34), in Hall (1992b: 114)

considerable academic and applied interest. Their subtitle was in itself revealing: *How Great Expectations in Washington are Dashed in Oakland; or, Why it's Amazing that Federal Programs Work at All, This Being the Saga of the Economic Development Administration as Told by Two Sympathetic Observers Who Seek to Build Morals on a Foundation of Ruined Hopes.* The growth in attention given to studies of policy implementation in the last two decades has, in part, also led to an increase in interest in policy evaluation. If we accept Lindblom's (1980: 64) notion that 'Most, perhaps all, administrative acts make or change policy in the process of trying to implement it' then this observation in itself justifies the need for monitoring and evaluation.

By incorporating monitoring and evaluation at the very beginning and throughout the tourism policy-making process, the type of information required from monitoring and evaluation can be specified during the formation of the policy and in advance of the policy's implementation. Therefore, the extent to which an option is capable of being evaluated could in fact be made one of the criteria for selection of policy options. Moreover, the policy analysis approach to evaluation, which acknowledges the politics of tourism public policy, is not simply concerned with carrying out technically correct evaluations; it has to be concerned with how evaluation results are ordered, consumed and utilised (Hogwood and Gunn 1984). Therefore, the findings of evaluation studies will be affected by such factors as:

• the clarity and specifics of tourism policy aims and objectives;
• prevailing government priorities;
• changes in government;
• demographic and population trends;
• changes in industry expectations and needs;
• interest group reactions (acceptance or opposition) and the degree to which they can exert themselves in the policy process;
• influences from community leaders, the mass media, and other powerful forces of change from the local level upwards;
• changes in local community or visitor needs.

'The most useful policy evaluation for policy-makers and administrators, and policy critics who wish to have a more solid basis for their positions, is the systematic evaluation that tries to determine cause-and-effect relationships and rigorously measure the impact of public policy' (Anderson 1984: 139). The design and operationalisation of monitoring and evaluation programmes involve clashes of values and interests which may stem from: (1) decisions as to why, when, what and how to evaluate, and (2) the selection of individuals and agencies to undertake the evaluation exercise. Monitoring and evaluation are often political tasks and so are closely linked to the political system. Nevertheless, evaluation is often mistakenly seen to be a rational, value-neutral task.

A model for policy evaluation – the importance of evaluation as an ongoing task

Evaluation research assumes at least some element of rationality to decision-making in that it has application to every kind of problem situation (see Chadwick 1971). In Graycar's (1983) policy evaluation model, four issues are seen to be paramount: conceptual issues, measurement issues, operational issues and political issues (Figure 6.1). Each issue is discussed briefly in turn.

Conceptual issues

Conceptual issues arise because of the nature or content and intended consequences of tourism policy, and the extent to which any evaluative

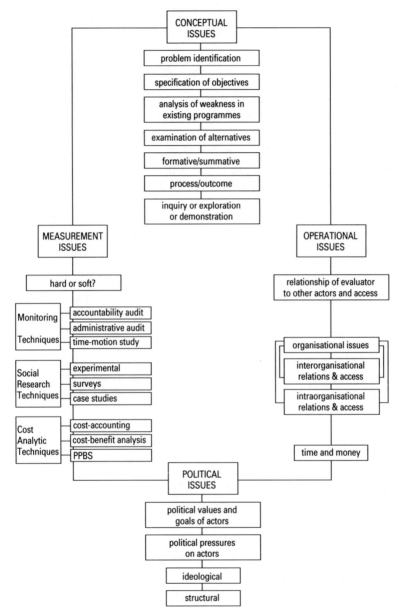

Figure 6.1 Evaluation model

Source: Graycar (1983: 165)

study is directed by those underwriting the evaluation. An evaluator may be required to investigate, within limited or expansive guidelines, an existing policy. He/she may be required to formulate an alternative policy or determine policy guidelines to improve policy. Whatever the terms of reference, evaluators must conceptualise the policy problem in terms of those with an interest in the policy (e.g. policy-makers, interest groups and those directly or indirectly affected). Other factors affecting the conceptualisation of the problem are:

- whether the evaluation is to be formative (undertaken while the policy is in process) or summative (undertaken when the policy in question is terminated, or the project is deemed to have been completed);
- whether the evaluation is to be one of process (which implies ongoing monitoring and feedback) or one of outcome and impact (which implies an assessment which relates outcomes and impacts to objectives);
- the extent to which the investigation is to gather data on problems, identify relationships between problems, and attitudes towards problems;
- whether information is to be provided on potential and actual implementation strategies, and with or without a commitment to action; and
- whether there is to be some demonstration as to the effectiveness of implementation strategies, and again whether there is to be or not to be a consequent commitment to action.

Measurement issues

The central issue concerning measurement is the degree of emphasis to be given to hard (quantitative) and soft (qualitative) data, though these 'are not mutually exclusive' (Graycar 1983: 170). According to Carter and Wharf (1973, in Graycar 1983), the three main areas into which evaluation research falls, include:

- monitoring techniques which involve a direct review of policy or programme objectives;
- social research techniques which are designed to contribute to knowledge of the policy problem and of the policy itself; and
- cost-analytical techniques which determine the value of the policy in terms of its benefits and costs or cost effectiveness (i.e. cost

accounting, cost–benefit analysis, and planning programme and budgeting systems).

In attempting to assess the social impacts of tourism planning and development, for instance, tourism and recreation planners and others have inherited the above techniques from other disciplinary areas and adapted them to their own needs.

Operational issues

According to Graycar (1983), the operational problems involved in mounting an evaluation are threefold: the relationship of the evaluator to all actors, organisational problems, and limited time and money. Each of these is dealt with briefly.

Evaluation, by its very nature, is often seen to be an exercise in confrontation (Hall and McArthur 1993) and is therefore a threatening activity. Judgements will reflect on individuals and agencies. An evaluator clearly requires much skill and sensitivity 'when dealing with sponsors, planners, administrators, field workers, support workers, recipients and any other actors' (Graycar 1983: 172).

Organisational problems are likely to occur as the evaluator attempts to access relevant and often very sensitive information from documents and from individuals by way of discussions or interviews. These, too, are threatening activities. The values, interests and positioning of the evaluator will also raise problems which arise as political issues (see below).

Evaluations are expensive and time-consuming. The evaluator may be deliberately constrained by the sponsor (or underwriter) through the latter's exercising control over time and money. 'By the same token, the evaluator can blame insufficient time and/or money for inadequacies in the study' (Graycar 1983: 172).

Political issues

Instead of reaching 'solutions' that can be judged by standards of rationality, policy making reaches settlements, reconciliations, adjustments, and agreements that one can evaluate only inconclusively by such standards as fairness, acceptability, openness to reconsideration and responsiveness to a variety of interests. And analysis in large part is transformed from an evaluative technique into a method of exerting influence, control and power which we call partisan analysis.

(Lindblom 1980: 122)

Policy evaluations are political, and 'Political problems are at the centre of any evaluation, because the decisions to be made on the basis of the evaluation [and indeed during the evaluation] are such that they fit into the political arena' (Graycar 1983: 172). The people and their organisations under review in association with the policy will probably raise such questions as:

- Who is evaluating the policy and why is the policy being evaluated?
- What are the values, interests and expectations of the evaluator?
- If the study is not an independent one, who is underwriting the evaluation, and what are their values, interests and expectations?
- What are the potential outcomes of the evaluation in terms of resource allocations, policy maintenance or termination, and, ultimately, agency activity?

A skilled evaluator will therefore take into account the political aims underlying the policy and analyse the extent to which the political system affects evaluation, and how the findings might be interpreted by those with a vested interest, and with the power to implement or brush aside those findings.

The politics of tourism policy: implications for monitoring and evaluation

A positive advantage of evaluation would be to depoliticise a situation, to provide a cold rational appraisal of policy alternatives or policies *per se* outside the steam heat of emotion and ideology. Sadly, this is very much a false hope, a product of technocracy and scientism pushed forward by those who hanker after a managerial outlook and who fail to appreciate that there is really no such thing as an apolitical arena.

(Jenkins 1978: 228)

Tourism policy monitoring and evaluation are complex and varied tasks. Jenkins and Sorensen (1994), for instance, argued that it was difficult to assess the merits of government investments in regional tourism development and other such programmes, not least because their effects:

- may be very long term (see Hogwood and Gunn 1984);
- may be quite small, low key and incremental;
- could be magnified through multiplier effects and the impact of other policies and programmes (each of whose impacts are very difficult to measure) (see Hogwood and Gunn 1984);
- may be in terms of individual and community morale, happiness and contentment (all of which are essentially unmeasurable), and general business management and leadership competencies. Such factors will affect other development activities over the longer term;
- will often be substantially influenced by a vast number of exogenous factors, many of which are beyond the control of any government;
- involve opportunity costs which are difficult to measure. Nevertheless, they are rarely taken into account in public policy evaluation.

For all these reasons, the impacts of tourism policies will be difficult to assess (also see Hogwood and Gunn 1984). There is also a real possibility that many tourism policies will be deemed to have failed if they are assessed simply in terms of their primary objectives, yet they may have generated positive benefits overall.

Policy evaluation should occur throughout the policy process. Policy evaluation may be inexpensive and involve as little as individuals reading documents and thinking about policy implementation and outcomes. At another extreme, it may also be very expensive and comprehensive involving an internal, external or combination of consulting teams. Policy evaluation is therefore concerned with trying to determine the process and impact of policy in real-life political conditions.

Monitoring and evaluation of tourism policies are not of neutral stuff. Above all other considerations, they are ultimately political tasks. Tourism policy objectives may be vague (and quite deliberately so), and the intended outcomes may not be explicit. Monitoring is much more than information collection and dissemination. According to Hogwood and Gunn (1984), monitoring

> requires decisions about what action will be taken if performance deviated unduly from what is desired. Thus monitoring is about control and the exercise of power. Those involved in programme delivery will be [and if they are not they should be!] aware of this, and this may affect how information about programme delivery is passed up to superiors. For managerial and political reasons governments may be

unwilling to take the action which the monitoring information would otherwise indicate.

(Hogwood and Gunn 1984: 221)

Policy-makers may use monitoring and evaluation to delay decisions and actions; to justify and legitimate decisions and actions already taken; to pass the buck; to vindicate the programme in the eyes of its constituents, its funders, or the public; to satisfy specified conditions (Weiss 1973, in Graycar 1983). Evaluations may thus be 'motivated by self service as well as public service, by a desire to use analysis as ammunition for partisan political purposes' (Anderson 1984: 135). As such, evaluations may even be undertaken to do little more than allay the fears of a few key interests, to defuse situations, to appear efficient, or to delay the political system.

Those who undertake evaluations of tourism policy would do well to recount Graycar's (1983) statement that:

It cannot be stressed too strongly that in the initial conceptualization of the evaluation, one must identify programme aims in terms of the politics of the actors, with thoughts turning to who might win, who might lose, how, and why. Any social development programme involves the distribution of status, influence and authority within a power context. This is the stuff of politics, especially when one considers that many programmes try to maintain a high level of public visibility and invariably are subject to pressures of all sorts from many directions.

(Graycar 1983: 173)

Summary

The policy-making process is not complete after a policy is implemented. A facet of the policy-making process (and a potentially very political one at that) is the monitoring and evaluation of outcomes against expectations or intended outcomes. In reality, it is a rare thing to see tourism policies critically evaluated, for this requires the commitment of substantial resources, and may pose a considerable threat to various interests in the policy-making process in an arena which is becoming increasingly politicised.

Evaluation does not conclude the tourism policy process. That process is ongoing. Policies and programmes continue (usually in some altered state) or are terminated. If they are terminated, they are replaced in the sense that the resources they tied up are given to some other policy or programme. Some stakeholders will voice concerns about the termination of the policy and their claims may be met, if not entirely. There is no clear beginning or end to policy-making.

Questions for review and discussion

1 What is evaluation?
2 Why are monitoring and evaluation important tasks?
3 Why are monitoring and evaluation political tasks?
4 What are some of the reasons why governments give little recognition to policy monitoring and evaluation?

Guide to further reading

The literature on policy evaluation is extensive, but scant with specific reference to tourism. Thus, Rossi *et al.* (1979), Graycar (1983), Hogwood and Gunn (1984), Hollick (1993) and Owen (1993) are suggested as excellent general overviews of policy (or programme) evaluation. The first three of the above readings also serve as a useful introduction to more detailed discussions of evaluative techniques which are taken up by such authors as Hollick (1993) and Owen (1993). Readers should consult Hall and McArthur (1993) for applications of evaluation in tourism (i.e. visitor management).

7
Studying tourism policy

'Policy is not a self-evident, independent behaviour fact. Policy acquires meaning because an observer perceives and interprets a course of actions amid the confusions of a complex world' [Heclo 1974: 4]. If public policy is the choices (intended and unintended) acted upon within a society, then public policy analysis becomes a method for disentangling those decisions, for exploring why issues arise on the agenda, and how they are resolved. Public policy analysis therefore requires us to 'puzzle out' (to use another apt phrase from Heclo) this interaction of values, interests and resources, specify how they are shaped by prevailing organisational arrangements and explore the way politics can intervene to confirm or upset the expected result.

(Davis *et al.* 1993: 16)

Policy-making is a political process. In this book we have attempted to provide a critical context for the study of tourism public policies. Emphasis has been given to the need to study policy at a number of levels, and for students of tourism to recognise the inherently political nature of tourism and tourism studies.

The purpose of this chapter is to examine some of the research implications arising from the earlier chapters. In particular, we see the need for more innovative research that penetrates the political system or 'black box' of decision-making. In other words, research that does more than describe the inputs and outputs of tourism policy-making. Figure

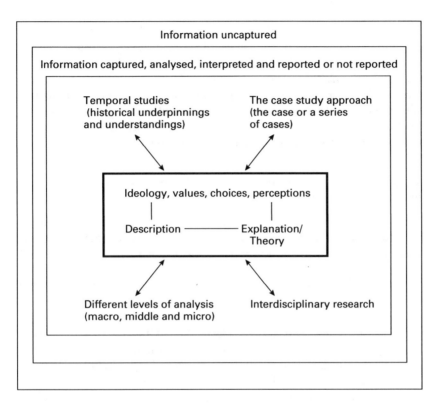

Figure 7.1 A conceptual framework for studying tourism public policy

7.1 provides a flexible framework for the study of tourism public policy. Four key methodological elements are identified in Figure 7.1. First, students should analyse public policy at a number of levels (macro, middle and micro) over time and space. Second, the historical imprint of earlier decisions, actions, procedures and programmes cannot be ignored. A short-term account of the public policy process might provide misleading findings. Third, the case study approach can offer a number of opportunities and constraints, and is discussed in more detail below. A fourth methodological consideration is the linking of description, theory and explanation, and the explicit recognition of ideology and values, an issue which has been highlighted throughout this book. As one or more of the four methodological approaches are omitted, the explanatory powers of any study will be weakened.

Although the policy information field is wide and impossible to encompass in its entirety, the values of the researcher surround all that is done in the course of a study. Subsequent to available information, the values of any researcher set the boundaries to information sources, methodology, analysis, and findings. The researcher may also influence who has access to the research, and the sources he/she cites may be politically motivated. Some, perhaps much, information will remain uncaptured, will not be detected or will not be accessible.

Integrating the macro, meso and micro levels of policy studies

Tourism, by its very nature, is a fractured and ill-defined policy arena. In comparison with other industry sectors, such as manufacturing and communications, tourism policy has been plagued with theoretical and methodological challenges.

At the macro level there is widespread ignorance of institutional arrangements and, particularly, the role of the state in tourism public policy. At the meso level there is little understanding of how and why decisions are made and actions are taken. At the micro level understanding of the relationship between individuals, their values and interests, and organisations and the state is lacking. Studies of tourism public policy at all three levels are made difficult by several considerations which have been discussed in earlier chapters. First, the problem of 'partial industrialisation' (Leiper 1990) which relates, in part, to the difficulty of defining a tourist industry where many of the actors and agencies crucial to the functioning of that industry actually work within or on the boundaries of other industries (e.g. transport). Second, the political system or 'black box' of decision-making which is not well understood in the tourism public policy arena, but which has been illuminated by studies in other policy arenas. Tourism systems transcend national, state and local boundaries, industries, government departments, and many other factors which impinge on policy analysis. Tracking down individuals and agencies involved in large policy decisions and actions may well be an arduous task. Third, is the need to not just pursue the study of tourism policy-making at different levels, but to actually integrate the levels of analysis.

Given the complex and dynamic nature of tourism policy-making it is essential for students of tourism to develop a clear understanding of the forces which shape tourism policy, planning and development.

We have argued that the key concepts of each chapter – institutional arrangements, values, interests, power, and evaluation – are the keys to opening the 'black box' of decision-making in any tourism public policy environment. Moreover, each concept provides opportunities for linking the different levels, elements and components of a fragmented industry. The concepts can be universally applied to studies of tourism public policy. The application of such concepts, which have been successfully applied in other policy arenas, will greatly assist our understanding of the tourism policy arena.

Studying tourism public policy

As noted throughout the book, despite the importance of tourism public policy as an area of research, there are few detailed studies of the tourism policy-making process. There is clearly a need for studies to develop a body of knowledge concerning tourism policy. The development of research approaches, analytical techniques, and models of tourism policy-making are crucial, particularly if we are to advance our understanding of government decisions and actions.

The decisions and actions of various actors and agencies, and systems of political management are complex and require a corresponding rich detail in their analysis (Barrett and Fudge 1981). Researchers should look to penetrate beyond assertions that bureaucrats are simply public servants rather than policy-makers. Extensive and prolonged contact with particular authorities and groups of professional officers is required to gain the cooperation needed to gather details of policy-making. In other words, performance in policy analysis 'depends crucially on an intimate knowledge of materials and tools, and on a highly personal relationship between the agent and his task' (Majone 1989: 45). This is particularly important in complex policy arenas operating over a long period of time where numerous actors have entrenched positions, and where the values, perceptions, decisions and actions of key interests were not previously documented.

Case studies provide a ready means to assist in the understanding of the tourism policy environment. As Anderson (1984) argued

Case studies . . . have a variety of uses. They can be employed to test existing theories, to provide detailed analysis of particular events, to analyze deviant cases that run counter to our generalizations, and to help provide an intuitive feel for the subtleties and nuances of the policy process and the practice of politics. Both case studies and more broadly conceived studies are needed in policy analysis.

(Anderson 1984: 165)

The case study approach has been well utilised in the policy studies field, but few comprehensive tourism policy studies have been undertaken. Case studies are developed and defined in such a way as to permit the researcher to use intricate details and methods for examining policy arenas and assessing the plausibility, and sometimes the general applicability, of theoretical developments. However, case studies are frequently criticised (Davis 1981; Sproats 1983; also see Mitchell 1989) on the basis that:

- they do not lend themselves to generalisation;
- they are difficult to remove from their own detail;
- they are generally not applied in a sufficiently scientific way to advance theory; and
- they rely upon historical, descriptive chronology and lack consistency in scope, context and conceptual cohesiveness.

On the other hand, Hall *et al.* (1975) outlined three areas in which case studies have substantial merit as explanatory tools:

- they help in understanding how policy develops;
- they help where there is considerable scale and complexity in policy tasks; and,
- they identify the purposive behaviour of the actors involved; that is, why decisions were made.

The concept of the case study is a basic feature of social science. Ragin (1993) identified four general approaches to case-based research. Those approaches are based on two dichotomies in which cases are conceived in terms of: (1) whether they are considered to be empirical units or theoretical constructs; and (2) whether they are understood as examples of general phenomena or as specific phenomena. The approach adopted affects the research method and conclusions. Approaches may not conform to those specified by Ragin. For example, hybrid approaches are very common because much social science research is based on a multitude of empirical and theoretical definitions and concepts. Indeed, hybrid approaches which utilise a number of key concepts to analyse tourism policy may even be more valuable because of the richness of their detail and explanatory power. Criticising a case study purely on the superficial notion that it is a one-off exercise is fruitless. Such criticism leads to a limited understanding and vision both of social life and social science (Ragin 1993). Case studies meet the maxim that 'ideas need to be tested against local experience' (Davis *et al.* 1993: 16). And each study must be assessed in terms of the manner in which that study has been crafted, the explanatory power of its arguments, and its contribution to our knowledge of tourism policy. As Majone and Quade (1980) point out:

An analysis is adequate if it meets the particular tests that are appropriate to the nature, context, and characteristic(s)… of the problem. But the process leading from the initial formulation to the implementation of a recommended solution is so complex that a global test is quite impossible. Rather the analysis must be broken down into distinct components, each of which will be tested for adequacy.

(Majone and Quade 1980: 2)

Between the lines

'Because the study of policy making is the study of all of politics from a particular point of view, reading on any aspects of politics will strengthen the student's understanding of policy making' (Lindblom 1980: 125). Therefore, like Lindblom (1980: 125), we too have been highly selective in making suggestions on what aspects of politics will strengthen students' understanding of tourism policy-making.

We do not claim that this book is the 'be all and end all' of the study of tourism policy. This book is only an introduction to the field, and is in itself a political tool. This book reflects our values, interests and arguments with respect to the study of tourism public policy. Tourism public policy, and its study, is a never-ending process of debate. We hope that this book clarifies and contributes to this debate.

Questions for review and discussion

1 What are the advantages and disadvantages of case studies of tourism public policy for the development of theory?
2 Is policy studies an art or a science?
3 How can a tourism policy study be judged as adequate?
4 How might your personal values affect the manner in which you conduct tourism public policy research?

Bibliography

Airey, D. (1984) 'Tourism administration in the USA', *Tourism Management 5*, 4: 269–279.

Albrow, M. (1970) *Bureaucracy*, London: Macmillan.

Allison, G. (1971) *The Essence of Decision*, Boston: Little, Brown.

Anderson, C.W. (1976) *Statecraft: An Introduction to Political Choice and Judgement*, New York: Wiley.

Anderson, J.E. (1984) *Public Policy Making*, 3rd edn, New York: CBS College Publishing.

Atkinson, M. and Chandler, M. (1983) *The Politics of Canadian Public Policy*, Toronto: University of Toronto Press.

Australian Bureau of Transport and Communications Economics and Jarden Morgan NZ Limited (1991) *Costs and Benefits of a Single Australasian Aviation Market*, Canberra: Australian Government Publishing Service.

Bachrach, P. (1969–70) 'A power analysis', *Public Policy* 18: 155–186.

Bachrach, P. and Baratz, M.S. (1962) 'Two faces of power', *American Political Science Review* 56, 4: 947–952.

Bachrach, P. and Baratz, M.S. (1963) 'Decisions and nondecisions: an analytical framework', *American Political Science Review* 57: 641–651.

Bachrach, P. and Baratz, M.S. (1970) *Power and Poverty, Theory and Practice*, New York: Oxford University Press.

Barrett, S. and Fudge, C. (1981) *Policy and Action*, London: Methuen.

Berry, J.M. (1989) 'Subgovernments, issue networks, and political conflict', in R.A. Harris and S.M. Milkis (eds) *Remaking American Politics*, Boulder: Westview Press.

Boyer, C. (1988) 'The return of aesthetics to city planning', *Society* 25, 4: 49–56.

Boyer, M.C. (1992) 'Cities for sale: merchandising history at South Street Seaport', in M. Sorkin (ed.) *Variations on a Theme Park: The New American City and the End of Public Space*, New York: Hill and Wang.

Bramham, P., Henry, I., Mommaas, H. and van der Poel, H. (1989) *Leisure and Urban Processes: Critical Studies of Leisure Policy in Western European Cities*, London: Routledge.

Britton, S.G. (1991) 'Tourism, capital and place: towards a critical geography of tourism', *Environment and Planning D: Society and Space*, 9, 4: 451–478.

Brooks, S. (1993) *Public Policy in Canada*, Toronto: McClelland and Stewart.

Brown, L.B. (1973) *Ideology*, Harmondsworth: Penguin.

Bull, A. (1991) *The Economics of Travel and Tourism*, Melbourne: Longman Cheshire.

Burbury, R. (1991) 'Profile: Simon Baggs', *B & T*, 30 August: 14, 21.

Cater, E. and Lowman, G. (eds) (1994) *Ecotourism: A Sustainable Option?*, London: John Wiley in association with the Royal Geographical Society.

Chadwick, G. (1971) *A Systems View of Planning*, Pergamon.

Chamberlain, J. (1992) 'On the tourism trail', *North and South*, September: 88–98.

Cheyne-Buchanan, J. (1992) 'The restructuring of government involvement in tourism in New Zealand 1987–1992', Unpublished Master of Business Studies report, Palmerston North: Massey University.

Cigler, A.J. (1985) 'Special interests and the policy process', *Policy Studies Journal* 14: 318–325.

Cigler, A.J. (1991) 'Interest groups: a subfield in search of an identity', in W. Crotty (ed.) *Political Science: Looking to the Future, Vol. 4, American Institutions*, Evanston: Northwestern University Press.

Cigler, A.J. and Loomis, B.A. (eds) (1986) *Interest Group Politics*, 2nd edn, Washington, DC: CQ Press.

Cohen, E. (1977) 'Toward a sociology of international tourism', *Social Research* 39, 1: 164–182.

Cohen, M.P. (1988) *The History of the Sierra Club 1892–1970*, San Francisco: Sierra Club Books.

Coleman, W.D. and Skogstad, G. (eds) (1990) *Policy Communities and Public Policy in Canada: A Structural Approach*, Toronto: Copp Clark Pitman.

Colgate, G. (ed.)(1982) *National Trade and Professional Associations of the United States*, Washington, DC: Columbia Books.

Compton, P.A. (1991) 'Hungary', in D.R. Hall (ed.) *Tourism and Economic Development in Eastern Europe and the Soviet Union*, London: Belhaven Press.

Craig-Smith, S. and French, C. (1994) *Learning to Live with Tourism*, Melbourne: Longman.

Craik, J. (1990) 'A classic case of clientelism: the Industries Assistance Commission Inquiry into Travel and Tourism', *Culture and Policy* 2, 1: 29–45.

Craik, J. (1991) *Resorting to Tourism: Cultural Policies for Tourist Development in Australia*, North Sydney: Allen and Unwin.

Crenson, M.A. (1971) *The Unpolitics of Air Pollution: A Study of Non-decisionmaking in the Cities*, Baltimore: Johns Hopkins Press.

Crick, M. (1989) 'Representations of international tourism in the social sciences: sun, sex, sights, savings, and servility', *Annual Review of Anthropology* 18: 307–344.

Crozier, M. (1964) *The Bureaucratic Phenomenon*, Chicago: University of Chicago Press.

Cunningham, G. (1963) 'Policy and Practice', *Public Administration* 41: 229–237.

Dahl, R.A. (1958) 'A critique of the ruling elite model', *American Political Science Review* 52, 2: 463–469.

Dahl, R.A. (1961) *Who Governs? Democracy and Power in an American City*, New Haven: Yale University Press.

Dahl, R.A. (1967) *Pluralist Democracy in the United States*, Chicago: Rand McNally.

Dahl, R.A. (1983) 'Comment on Manley', *American Political Science Review* 77, 2: 386–389.

Davis, B.W. (1981) 'Characteristics and Influence of the Australian Conservation Movement: An Examination of Selected Conservation Strategies', Unpublished Ph.D. Thesis, Department of Politics, University of Tasmania, Hobart.

Davis, G., Wanna, J., Warhurst, J. and Weller, P. (1993) *Public Policy in Australia*, 2nd edn, St Leonards: Allen and Unwin.

DeAngelis, R. and Parkin, A. (1980) 'Critiques of pluralism', in A. Parkin, J. Summers and D. Woodward (eds) *Government Politics and Power in Australia: An Introductory Reader*, Melbourne: Longman Cheshire.

deLeon, P. (1994) 'Democracy and the policy sciences: aspirations and operations', *Policy Studies Journal* 22, 2: 200–212.

Deutsch, K. (1970) *Politics and Government: How People Decide Their Fate*, Boston: Houghton Mifflin.

Dombrink, J. and Thompson, W. (1990) *The Last Resort: Success and Failure in Campaigns for Casinos*, Reno: University of Nevada Press.

Dye, T. (1978) *Understanding Public Policy*, 3rd edn, Englewood Cliffs, N.J.: Prentice-Hall.

Dye, T. (1992) *Understanding Public Policy*, 7th edn, Englewood Cliffs, N.J.: Prentice-Hall.

Easton, D. (1965) *A Framework for Political Analysis*, Englewood Cliffs, N.J.: Prentice-Hall.

Edgell, D. (1990) *International Tourism Policy*, New York: Van Nostrand Reinhold.

Eisinger, P.K. (1988) *The Rise of the Entrepreneurial State*, Madison: University of Wisconsin Press.

Etzioni, A. (1984) 'Foreword', in A. Majchrzak, *Methods for Policy Research*, Beverly Hills: Sage.

Fischer, F. (1990) *Technocracy and the Politics of Expertise*, Newbury Park: Sage Publications.

Fischer, F. and Forester, J. (eds) (1993) *The Argumentative Turn in Policy Analysis and Planning*, Durham: Duke University Press.

Fishkin, J.S. (1991) *Democracy and Deliberation: New Directions for Democratic Reform*, New Haven: Yale University Press.

Forester, J. (1988) *Planning in the Face of Power*, Berkeley: University of California Press.

Forester, J. (1993) *Critical Theory, Public Policy, and Planning Practice*, Albany: State University of New York Press.

Forward, R. (1974) 'Introduction', in R. Forward (ed.) *Public Policy in Australia*, Melbourne: Cheshire.

Foucault, M. (1972) *The Archeology of Knowledge*, trans. A.M. Sheridan Smith, New York: Pantheon.

Gallie, W.B. (1955–56) 'Essentially contested concepts', *Proceedings of the Aristotelian Society* 56: 167–198.

Goleman, D. (1992) 'Architects rediscover the best city planners: citizens', *New York Times*, 19 June: B5, B9.

Gordon, I., Lewis, J. and Young, K. (1977) 'Perspectives on policy analysis', *Public Administration Bulletin* 25: 26–35.

Graycar, A. (1983) *Welfare Politics in Australia*, Melbourne: Macmillan.

Gunn, C.A. (1994) *Tourism Planning*, 3rd edn, Washington: Taylor and Francis.

Gunn, L. and Hogwood, B. (1982) *Models of Policy-Making*, Strathclyde: Centre for the Study of Public Policy, University of Strathclyde.

Hall, C.M. (1992a) *Wasteland to World Heritage: Preserving Australia's Wilderness*, Carlton: Melbourne University Press.

Hall, C.M. (1992b) *Hallmark Tourist Events: Impacts, Management and Planning*, London: Belhaven Press.

Hall, C.M. (1994a) *Tourism and Politics: Policy, Power and Place*, London: Belhaven Press.

Hall, C.M. (1994b) *Tourism in the Pacific Rim: Development Impacts and Markets*, Melbourne: Longman.

Hall, C.M. (1995) *Introduction to Tourism in Australia: Impacts, Planning and Development*, 2nd edn, Melbourne: Longman Cheshire.

Hall, C.M. and McArthur, S. (eds) (1993) *Heritage Management in New Zealand and Australia: Visitor Management, Interpretation and Marketing*, Auckland: Oxford University Press.

Hall, D.R. (ed.) (1991a) *Tourism and Economic Development in Eastern Europe and the Soviet Union*, London: Belhaven Press.

Hall, D.R. (1991b) 'Introduction', in D.R. Hall (ed.), *Tourism and Economic Development in Eastern Europe and the Soviet Union*, London: Belhaven Press.

Hall, D.R. (1991c) 'Contemporary challenges', in D.R. Hall (ed.) *Tourism and Economic Development in Eastern Europe and the Soviet Union*, London: Belhaven Press.

Hall, P. (1975) *Urban and Regional Planning*, Middlesex: Penguin.

Hall, P. (1982) *Urban and Regional Planning*, 2nd edn, Middlesex: Penguin.

Hall, P., Land, H., Parker, R. and Webb, A. (1975) *Change, Choice and Conflict in Social Policy*, London: Heinemann.

Ham, C. and Hill, M. (1984) *The Policy Process in the Modern Capitalist State*, New York: Harvester Wheatsheaf.

Harrison, D. (ed.) (1992) *Tourism and the Less Developed Countries*, London: Belhaven Press.

Harvey, D. (1993) 'From space to place and back again: reflections on the condition of postmodernity', in J. Bird, B. Curtis, T. Putnam, G. Robertson and L. Tickner (eds) *Mapping the Futures: Local Cultures, Global Change*, London and New York: Routledge.

Hawker, G., Smith, R.F.I. and Weller, P. (1979) *Politics and Policy in Australia*, St Lucia: University of Queensland Press.

Hayes, B.J. (1981) 'The congressional travel and tourism caucus and US national tourism policy', *International Journal of Tourism Management*, June: 121–137.

Haynes, P. (1973) 'Towards a concept of monitoring', *Town Planning Review*, 45, 1.

Haywood, K.M. (1988) 'Responsible and responsive tourism planning in the community', *Tourism Management* 9, 2: 105–118.

Heclo, H. (1972) 'Review article: policy analysis', *British Journal of Political Science* 2, 1: 83–108.

Heclo, H. (1974) *Modern Social Politics in Britain and Sweden*, New Haven: Yale University Press.

Heclo, H. (1978) 'Issue networks and the executive establishment', in A. King (ed.) *Annual Review of Energy, Vol. 4*, Palo Alto: Annual Reviews Inc.

Henning, D.H. (1974) *Environmental Policy and Administration*, New York: American Elsevier Publishing Company.

Henry, I. and Bramham, P. (1986) 'Leisure, the local state and social order', *Leisure Studies* 5: 189–209.

Hewison, R. (1988) 'Great expectations-hyping heritage', *Tourism Management* 9, 3: 239–240.

Hogwood, B. and Gunn, L. (1984) *Policy Analysis for the Real World*, Oxford: Oxford University Press.

Hollick, M. (1993) *An Introduction to Project Evaluation*, Melbourne: Longman Cheshire.

Hollinshead, K. (1992) '"White" gaze, "red" people – shadow visions: the disidentification of "Indians" in cultural tourism', *Leisure Studies* 11: 43–64.

Hughes, H.L. (1984) 'Government support for tourism in the UK: a different perspective', *Tourism Management* 5, 1: 13–19.

Industries Assistance Commission (1989a) *Draft Report on Travel and Tourism*, Canberra: Australian Government Publishing Service.

Industries Assistance Commission (1989b) *Travel and Tourism, Report No. 423*, Canberra: Australian Government Publishing Service.

Inskeep, E. (1991) *Tourism Planning: An Integrated and Sustainable Development Approach*, New York: Van Nostrand Reinhold.

IUOTO (International Union of Official Travel Organizations) (1974) 'The role of the state in tourism', *Annals of Tourism Research*, 1, 3: 66–72.

Jeffries, D. (1989) 'Selling Britain – a case for privatisation?', *Travel and Tourism Analyst* 1: 69–81.

Jenkins, J.M. (1993a) 'Tourism policy in rural New South Wales: policy and research priorities', *Geojournal*, 29, 3: 281–290.

Jenkins, J.M. (1993b) 'An alternative economic base: tourism and recreation development and management', in A.D. Sorensen and W.R. Epps (eds) *Prospects and Policies for Rural Australia*, Melbourne: Longman Cheshire.

Jenkins, J.M. (1994) 'Rural recreation and tourism: policy and planning', in D. Mercer (ed.) *New Viewpoints in Australian Outdoor Recreation Research and Planning*, Williamstown: Hepper Marriott and Associates.

Jenkins, J.M. and Sorensen, A.D. (1994) 'Tourism, regional development and the Commonwealth Department of Tourism', Paper presented at the Institute of Australian Geographers' Conference, Magnetic Island, September.

Jenkins, W.I. (1978) *Policy Analysis: A Political and Organisational Perspective*, London: Robertson.

Kelly, M. and McConville, C. (1991) 'Down by the docks', in G. Davison and C. McConville (eds) *A Heritage Handbook*, North Sydney: Allen and Unwin.

Kosters, M. (1984) 'The deficiencies of tourism science without political science: comment on Richter', *Annals of Tourism Research* 11: 610–612.

Lasswell, H.D. (1936) *Politics: Who Gets What, When, How?* New York: McGraw-Hill.

Lea, J. (1988) *Tourism and Development in the Third World*, London: Routledge.

Lefebvre, H. (1991) *The Production of Space*, Oxford: Basil Blackwell.

Leiper, N. (1979) 'The framework of tourism: towards a definition of tourism, tourist, and the tourist industry', *Annals of Tourism Research* 6, 4: 390–407.

Leiper, N. (1989) *Tourism and Tourism Systems, Occasional Paper No. 1*, Palmerston North: Department of Management Systems, Massey University.

Leiper, N. (1990) *Tourism Systems: An Interdisciplinary Perspective*, Palmerston North: Department of Management Systems, Business Studies Faculty, Massey University.

Lickorish, L.J., Jefferson, A., Bodlender, J and Jenkins, C.L. (1991) *Developing Tourism Destinations: Policies and Perspectives*, Harlow: Longman.

Lindblom, C.E. (1959) 'The science of muddling through', *Public Administration Review* 19: 79–88.

Lindblom, C.E. (1977) *Politics and Markets*, New York: Basic Books.

Lindblom, C.E. (1980) *The Policy-Making Process*, 2nd edn, Englewood-Cliffs, N.J.: Prentice-Hall.

Lowi, T. (1970) 'Decisionmaking versus policymaking: toward an antidote to technocracy', *Public Administration Review* 30, 3: 314–325.

Lukes, S. (1974) *Power: A Radical View*, London: Macmillan.

McCool, D. (1989) 'Subgovernments and the impact of policy fragmentation and accommodation', *Policy Studies Review* 8: 264–287.

McIntosh, R.W. and Goeldner, C.R. (1990) *Tourism Principles, Practices and Philosophies*, New York: John Wiley and Sons.

Machiavelli, N. (1988) *The Prince*, eds Q. Skinner and R. Price, Cambridge: Cambridge University Press.

Macintyre, B. (1994) 'Disney loses theme park battle', *Weekend Australian* 1–2 October: 16.

McKercher, B. (1993a) 'The unrecognized threat to tourism: can tourism survive sustainability', *Tourism Management* 14, 2: 131–136.

McKercher, B. (1993b) 'Australian conservation organisations' perspectives on tourism in National Parks: a critique', *Geojournal* 29, 3: 307–313.

Majone, G. (1980a) 'The uses of policy analysis', in B.H. Raven (ed.) *Policy Studies Review Annual* 4: 161–180, Beverly Hills: Sage

Majone, G. (1980b) 'An anatomy of pitfalls', in G. Majone and E.S. Quade (eds) *Pitfalls of Analysis*, Chichester: International Institute for Applied Systems Analysis/John Wiley and Sons.

Majone, G. (1989) *Evidence, Argument and Persuasion in the Policy Process*, New Haven and London: Yale University Press.

Majone, G. and Quade, E.S. (eds) (1980) *Pitfalls of Analysis*, Chichester: International Institute for Applied Systems Analysis/John Wiley and Sons.

March, J.G. and Olsen, J.P. (1989) *Rediscovering Institutions: The Organisation Basis of Politics*, New York: The Free Press.

Marsh, D. (1983) 'Interest group activity and structural power: Lindblom's politics and markets', in D. Marsh (ed.) *Capital and Politics in Western Europe*, London: Frank Cass.

Matthews, T. (1976) 'Interest group access to the Australian Government Bureaucracy', in *Royal Commission on Australian Government Administration: Appendixes to Report, Volume Two*, Canberra: Australian Government Publishing Service.

Matthews, T. (1980) 'Australian pressure groups', in H. Mayer and H. Nelson (eds) *Australian Politics A Fifth Reader*, Melbourne: Longman Cheshire.

Meleghy, T., Preglau, M. and Tafertshofer, A. (1985) 'Tourism development and value change', *Annals of Tourism Research* 12: 181–199.

Mellor, R.E.H. (1991) 'Eastern Germany (the former German Democratic Republic)', in D.R. Hall (ed.) *Tourism and Economic Development in Eastern Europe and the Soviet Union*, London: Belhaven Press.

Mercer, D. (1979) 'Victoria's land conservation council and the alpine region', *Australian Geographical Studies* 17, 1: 107–130.

Michaels, S. (1992) 'Issue networks and activism', *Policy Studies Review* 11, 3/4: 241–258.

Ministry of Tourism (1991) *Introducing the Ministry of Tourism*, Wellington: Ministry of Tourism.

Mitchell, B. (1989) *Geography and Resource Analysis*, Essex: Longman Scientific and Technical.

Molnar, J.J. and Rogers, D.L. (1982) 'Interorganisational coordination in environmental management: process, strategy and objectives', in D.E. Mann (ed.) *Environmental Policy Implementation*, Lexington: Lexington Books.

Mommaas, H. and van der Poel, H. (1989) 'Changes in economy, politics and lifestyles: an essay on the restructuring of urban leisure', in P. Bramham, I. Henry, H. Mommaas and H. van der Poel (eds) *Leisure and Urban Processes: Critical Studies of Leisure Policy in Western European Cities*, London: Routledge.

Moodie, G.C. and Studdert-Kennedy, R. (1970) *Opinions, Publics and Pressure Groups: An Essay on Vox Populi and Representative Government*, London: Allen and Unwin.

Morriss, P. (1972) 'Power in New Haven: a reassessment of "Who Governs?"', *British Journal of Political Science* 2, 4: 457–465.

Mucciaroni, G. (1991) 'Unclogging the arteries: the defeat of client politics and the logic of collective action', *Policy Studies Journal* 19, 3–4: 474–494.

Murphy, P.E. (1985) *Tourism: A Community Approach*, New York and London: Methuen.

Murphy, P.E. (1988) 'Community driven tourism planning', *Tourism Management* 9, 2: 96–104.

Nagel, S. (1990) 'Policy theory and policy studies', *Policy Studies Journal* 18, 4: 1046–1057.

Nelson, B. (1984) *Making an Issue of Child Abuse*. Chicago: The University of Chicago Press.

New South Wales Tourism Commission (1991) *Annual Report 1990–91*, Sydney: New South Wales Tourism Commission.

New Zealand Tourism Board (1991) *Tourism in New Zealand: A Strategy for Growth*, Wellington: New Zealand Tourism Board.

New Zealand Tourism Board (1992) *Tourism in the 90s*, Wellington: New Zealand Tourism Board.

New Zealand Tourism Board (1994) *International Visitor Arrivals to New Zealand – Summary*, Wellington: New Zealand Tourism Board.

New Zealand Tourism Department (1991) *Corporate Plan 1991/92*, Wellington: New Zealand Tourism Department.

Nordlinger, E. (1981) *On the Autonomy of the Democratic State*, Cambridge, Mass.: Harvard University Press.

Norkunas, M.K. (1993) *The Politics of Memory: Tourism, History, and Ethnicity in Monterey, California*, Albany: State University of New York Press.

O'Riordan, T. (1971) *Perspectives on Resource Management*, London: Pion.

OECD (1992) *Tourism Policy and International Tourism in OECD Countries*, Paris: OECD.

Ostrom, E. (1986) 'An agenda for the study of institutions', *Public Choice* 48: 3–25.

Owen, J.M. (1993) *Program Evaluation*, St Leonards: Allen and Unwin.

Pal, L.A. (1992) *Public Policy Analysis: An Introduction*, Scarborough: Nelson Canada.

Papson, S. (1981) 'Spuriousness and tourism: politics of two Canadian provincial governments', *Annals of Tourism Research* 8, 2: 220–235.

Pearce, D. (1987) *Tourism Today: A Geographical Analysis*, Harlow: Longman.

Pearce, D. (1989) *Tourist Development*, Harlow: Longman.

Pearce, D.G. (1992) *Tourist Organisations*, Harlow: Longman Scientific and Technical.

Peck, J.G. and Lepie, A.S. (1989) 'Tourism and development in three North Carolina coastal towns', in V. Smith (ed.) *Hosts and Guests: The Anthropology of Tourism*, 2nd edn, Philadelphia, University of Pennsylvania Press.

Pelissero, J.P., Henschen, B.M. and Sidlow, E.I. (1991), 'Urban regimes, sports stadiums, and the politics of economic development agendas in Chicago', *Policy Studies Review* 10, 2/3: 117–129.

Philippine Women's Research Collective (1985) *Filipinos for Sale: An Alternative Philippine Report on Women and Tourism*, Quezon City: Philippine Women's Research Collective.

Pressman, J.L. and Wildavsky, A.B. (1973) *Implementation*, Berkeley: University of California Press.

Quade, E.S. (1980) 'Pitfalls in formulation and modelling', in G. Majone and E.S. Quade (eds) *Pitfalls of Analysis*, Chichester: International Institute for Applied Systems Analysis/John Wiley and Sons.

Ragin, C.C. (1993) 'Introduction', in C.C. Ragin and H.S. Becker (eds) (1993) *What is a Case? Exploring the Foundations of Social Science Inquiry*, Cambridge: Cambridge University Press.

Ragin, C.C. and Becker, H.S. (eds) (1993) *What is a Case? Exploring the Foundations of Social Science Inquiry*, Cambridge: Cambridge University Press.

Richter, L.K. (1989) *The Politics of Tourism in Asia*, Honolulu: University of Hawaii Press.

Ripley, R.B. and Franklin, G.A. (1987) *Congress, the Bureaucracy, and Public Policy*, Homewood: Dorsey Press.

Roche, M. (1992) 'Mega-events and micro-modernization: on the sociology of the new urban tourism', *British Journal of Sociology*, 43, 4: 563–600.

Rokeach, M. (1973) *The Nature of Human Values*, New York: The Free Press.

Rossi, P.H., Freeman, H.E. and Wright, S.R. (1979) *Evaluation: A Systematic Approach*, Beverly Hills: Sage.

Ryan, C. (1991) *Recreational Tourism: A Social Science Perspective*, London and New York: Routledge.

Sabatier, P. (1987) 'Knowledge, policy-oriented learning, and policy change: an advocacy coalition framework', *Knowledge: Creation, Diffusion, Utilization* 1: 649–692.

Salisbury, R.H., Heinz, J.P., Laumann, E.O. and Nelson, R.L. (1987) 'Who works with whom? Interest group alliances and opposition', *American Political Science Review* 81: 1217–1234.

Schattschneider, E. (1960) *Semi-Sovereign People: A Realist's View of Democracy in America*, New York: Holt, Rinehart and Winston.

Schlozman, K.L. (1984) 'What accent and heavenly chorus? Political equality and the American pressure system', *Journal of Politics* 46: 1006–1032.

Schlozman, K.L. and Tierney, J.T. (1986) *Organized Interests and American Democracy*, New York: Harper and Row.

Scrutton, R. (1982) *A Dictionary of Political Thought*, London: Pan Books.

Self, P. (1985) *Political Theories of Modern Government, Its Role and Reform*, London: George Allen and Unwin.

Selin, S. and Beason, K. (1991) 'Interorganisational relations in tourism', *Annals of Tourism Research*, 18, 4: 639–652.

Shaw, G. and Williams, A.M. (1994) *Critical Issues in Tourism: A Geographical Perspective*, Oxford: Blackwell.

Simeon, R. (1976) 'Studying public policy', *Canadian Journal of Political Science*, 9, 4: 558–580

Simmons, R., Davis, B.W., Chapman, R.J.K. and Sager, D.D. (1974) 'Policy flow analysis: a conceptual model for comparative public policy research', *Western Political Quarterly* 27, 3: 457–468.

Simmons, R.H. and Dvorin, E.P. (1977) *Public Administration: Values, Policy and Change*, Port Washington: Alfred Publishing Co.

Smith, S.L.J. (1988) 'Defining tourism: a supply-side view', *Annals of Tourism Research* 15, 2: 179–190.

Spann, R.N. and Curnow, G.R. (eds) (1975) *Public Policy and Administration in Australia: A Reader*, Sydney: Wiley.

Sproats, K. (1983) 'A tale of two towns: policy and action in the Bathurst-Orange growth centre: a case of perceptions, politics and power in centrally commanded regional policy planning', Unpublished Ph.D. thesis, Armidale: University of New England.

Steinlieb, G. and Hughes, J. (1983) *The Atlantic City Gamble: A Twentieth Century Fund Report*, Cambridge: Harvard University Press.

Teske, P. and Sur, B. (1991) 'Winners and losers: politics, casino gambling, and development in Atlantic City', *Policy Studies Review* 10, 2/3: 130–137.

Urry, J. (1990) *The Tourist Gaze: Leisure and Travel in Contemporary Societies*, London: Sage Publications.

Vasil, A. (1992) 'Tourism Board lays off 40 staff', *The Dominion*, 27 February.

Vogel, D. (1989) *Fluctuating Fortunes: The Political Power of Business in America*, New York: Basic Books.

Warren, R.L., Rose, S.M. and Bergunder, A.F. (1974) *The Structure of Urban Reform*, Lexington, Mass.: D.C. Heath and Company.

Wildavsky, A. (1979) *Speaking Truth to Power*, New York: John Wiley.

Williams, A.M. and Shaw. G. (eds)(1988) *Tourism and Economic Development: Western European Experiences*, London: Belhaven Press.

Wilson, J. (1988) *Politics and Leisure*, Boston: Unwin Hyman.

Wilson, W. (1941) 'The study of administration', *Political Science Quarterly* 55: 481–506.

Wolfinger, R.E.C. (1971) 'Nondecisions and the study of local politics', *American Political Science Review* 65: 1063–1080.

Wong, G.M. (1985) 'Of franchise relocation, expansion and competition in professional sports teams: the ultimate political football?', *Seton Hall Legislative Journal* 9: 7–79.

Zeigler, H. (1980) 'Interest groups and public policy: a comparative, revisionist perspective', in R. Scott (ed.) *Interest Groups and Public Policy*, South Melbourne: Macmillan.

Name index

Place index

Subject index